Born in Kent in 1977, Ed Smith ....
School and Peterhouse, Cambridge, where he read History.
Having scored a hundred on his first-class debut, he went on to
play for Young England.

After leaving Cambridge he became a professional with
Kent, and he was awarded his county cap in 2001. He has
played cricket in Australia, India and in the ghetto of Compton,
Los Angeles.

Playing Hard Ball, his first book, was serialised by *The Times*.

'Smith has written an instructive and entertaining book, full of
the insights into the similarities – and differences – between the
two games and the cultures they represent' Hugh Massingberd,
Daily Telegraph

'Smith succeeds in recreating the colour and culture of baseball,
whether it is the obsession with statistics . . . or the vigour and
comedy of its vernacular' Nick Greenslade, *New Statesman*

'His assertion that the lot of cricket batsmen is analogous to that
of baseball's pitchers, and vice versa to hitters is inspired.
Similarly he makes thought-provoking comments on the 'science' of baseball as opposed to the 'art' of cricket' Chris Power,
The Times

'Smith's passion for baseball is well articulated, and he subjects
both games to intelligent scrutiny' Mike Marqusee, *Independent*

Playing
Hard Ball

E. T. SMITH

An *Abacus* Book

First published in Great Britain in 2002
by Little, Brown

This edition published by Abacus in 2003
Reprinted 2003, 2004

A CIP catalogue record for this book
is available from the British Library.

ISBN 0 349 11666 0

Typeset by M Rules
Printed and bound in Great Britain by
Clays Ltd, St Ives plc

Abacus
An imprint of
Time Warner Book Group UK
Brettenham House
Lancaster Place
London WC2E 7EN

www.twbg.co.uk

CONTENTS

For J. B. S.

ACKNOWLEDGEMENTS

Alan Samson and Becky Quintavalle, my editors at Little, Brown, not only improved the final version, but also shaped this project from the start. The book would have been impossible without them.

I am very grateful to everyone at the New York Mets for making me feel so welcome in both Florida and New York, particularly: Nelson and Sandra Doubleday, Duke Barnett, Steve Phillips, Omar Minaya, Bobby Valentine and, of course, all the players.

Thanks also to: Kathryn Heminway, without whose introduction I might never have gone to Spring Training in the first place; George Plimpton, for the books and the phone calls; Keith Blackmore, for giving me a ticket to the World Series and encouraging me to write for *The Times*; Rob Steen for passing on some good books and stories; and Clive Russell at Major League Baseball for being such a good baseball contrarian.

Tommy Caplan helped me with the initial idea for this book, and John Adamson, Woody Brock and Martin Trew clarified my thoughts by asking difficult questions. Bob Chisholm and Jonathan Smith read and commented on early drafts.

I couldn't have written this book without having places to stay and write in Manhattan. For that, and much else besides, I am indebted to Vikram, Alison, Aidan and Bill.

Above all, thanks to the Kent players for making the cricket part of this book so much fun.

E. T. S.

May 2002

PROLOGUE

It was always a soft ball, a tennis ball. At the age of three I would stand in front of the three lines chalked on to the garage door or in front of real cricket wickets on our bumpy lawn and Dad, Mum or my sister Becky would bowl at me. For hours on end. For catch or for cricket it was always a soft ball.

Then Jamie, a teenage boy who lived with us, let me try on his motorbike helmet. I stood on a chair in front of the mirror in his room and peered at myself. It was so big on me that I could hardly walk. But I picked up my bat and wobbled out of the door and stood in front of the garage and asked Dad to bowl at me with a hard ball. He wouldn't. But I wore him down. Looking troubled, he went into the house and came back with an old scuffed one. He held it up.

'Are you sure? A hard ball?'

'Yes.'

'It's hard, mind. It could hurt you.'

1
BASEBALL?
YOU MUST BE KIDDING

Cricket and baseball are like parents and their teenage children: they have so much in common and yet remain a total mystery to each other. The similarities are obviously profound: the isolation of pressure on an individual within the context of a team game; the duel between bat and ball; the rich, and often romanticised, aesthetic aspect of both sports; their capacity to inspire literary attention; the view that each is somehow more than just a game, a metaphysical symbol of something more important – America itself, or the British way of life.

And yet baseball fans – those who have heard of it – think cricket is a tedious, class-ridden English anachronism, 'baseball on Valium'. And cricket fans return the compliment by viewing baseball as a typically populist and vulgar American bastardisation of a minor English game played by girls.

Until recently I lined up wholeheartedly with the Brits in the cricket versus baseball debate. I used to consider American sport to be an introspective, nationalistic joke.

Super Bowl, World Championships, World Series – who were these Yanks trying to kid? No wonder an American team always won; only Americans played their damned sports.

Baseball scarcely even warranted a mention. My childhood friends were mostly cricketers, so baseball was tarred with the brush of rounders – a game for girls and wimps who were scared of hard cricket balls. Watching baseball, as everybody knew, was more boring than watching grass grow.

Nor was I much enamoured with America in general. Despite the fact that I had never set foot in the country, I used to laugh about gung-ho American nationalism, ghetto shoot-outs, paltry literacy levels and its all-pervasive litigiousness. I'd heard that 60 per cent of Americans couldn't name one of their senators; Ronald Reagan frequently answered a question entirely unrelated to the one he had been asked; Dan Quayle, his vice-president, couldn't spell 'potato', and an American woman, it was reported, had successfully sued a manufacturer of microwave ovens after she blew up her rain-drenched poodle by trying to dry it off with a few minutes on 'defrost'. Knocking the States as uncivilised was all so easy.

So what happened to me? How did I go from 'Americanophobe' and arch-baseball cynic to writing a book about America's 'national pastime'?

Chance played a big part. Although I was probably slowly changing my mind about America anyway, it was only when I made an unscheduled trip to New York that I started to understand what these Americans saw in their silly summer obsession. And the only reason I went to New York was because of a fateful cricket match.

*

In the summer of 1998 I was playing for the British Universities against South Africa at Fenners in Cambridge, a match I had been looking forward to for months. While I was batting in the second innings, on a pitch that I had come to know as placid and reliable, the fast bowler Steve Elworthy managed to find enough life and lift to hit me flush on the right hand. Broken – I knew it straightaway. I batted on badly for about twenty minutes before taking off my batting glove. One finger was twice the width of the others; once the glove is off you can never get it back on over the swollen finger.

That game and that particular dream were over: there would be no hundred for me against the touring side, just a broken finger and the certainty of missing a month's cricket with Kent, the county side I had been due to rejoin for the rest of the season.

In the taxi on the way to hospital I remembered something my history tutor had said to me the previous evening. 'If ever you get an unexpected week off,' he had offered, with donnish ignorance of the professional cricket season, 'buy a cheap flight to New York – it's a different world from anything you've ever seen up until now.'

Looking back, it seems absurdly spoilt – after one setback, immediately planning to get over it with an impromptu holiday – but I decided to ask my Kent coach, who would scarcely be able to find any use for me with a broken finger, if he minded if I went away for a few days. He agreed. On the condition that I went jogging in Central Park, looked after myself, and came back in plenty of time to get the necessary physiotherapy on my finger, I was free to fly. So I did.

After seven hours trapped in 'cattle class' with my right

hand suspended near my left ear, I was in serious need of being cheered up. The Manhattan skyline, in those days still adorned by the twin towers of the World Trade Center, would do the trick.

I'd seen the view, as everyone has, so many times before – not in real life, but in countless films, books and magazines. Manhattan's jagged silhouette, its skyscrapers improbably bunched like upturned matchboxes, has been reproduced so relentlessly that it is an inescapable part of our everyday aesthetic experience. In reality, it couldn't be that different, could it?

But it was. Manhattan might not be exactly beautiful from 10,000 feet, or even closer up, but the evident bravura self-confidence of building *that* on a tiny island only twelve miles long and five miles wide sent an electric charge down my spine. I had caught the New York buzz and I hadn't even touched down yet.

Since that first trip to New York, I have been back every year, staying for weeks or months at a time, and bored my friends at home with endless eulogies about New York's energy, eccentricity and Downtown scene. Nor have they failed to point out the irony of my sudden U-turn on America.

It might be forgivable, even inevitable, for an Englishman in his early twenties to fall in love with New York. But falling for baseball? Hardly. I am now used to English people asking me, just as I used to ask baseball fans, how I could possibly take seriously 'this rounders stuff'.

But it deserves to be taken seriously, not only as a great game, which it undoubtedly is, but also as a metaphor for America. The philosopher Jacques Barzun was surely exaggerating when he wrote, 'He who wants to understand the heart and soul of America must first understand baseball.' But only slightly. Baseball and America are as closely tied together as any other country and its national game.

Perhaps the timing of my first trips to the States helped me get hooked on baseball. The year 1998 was the summer baseball had been waiting for, the year of the legendary home run race between Sammy Sosa and Mark McGwire, who were both vying to break Roger Maris's season record of sixty-one runs. After decades of being overtaken by basketball and American football, baseball was putting itself back at the top of the sporting agenda, particularly in New York.

It was the summer the Yankees 'swept' (won 4-0, in layman's terms) the World Series, and even in July the city seemed to sense a triumphant season. I found myself loitering by the TVs in New York delis, fascinated by baseball words like *winningest* – 'Pettitte is the winningest pitcher in New York this year' – wondering if a pitcher would 'get out of an inning' despite the 'bases being loaded'. Everyone was into baseball. Perhaps it wasn't quite so bad after all.

Americans are great salesmen and the presence of a cricketer among them prompted them to try selling baseball. When I went to a store called Nobody Beats the Wiz, and the young black salesman found out I was an English cricketer, he immediately invited me to play baseball with him and his friends in Brooklyn. 'We'll have you playing baseball instead of that cricket stuff in no time!' he said, as he wrote down the name of the park in Brooklyn. That was typical of the way I was treated by vast numbers of supposedly 'cold and selfish' New Yorkers.

I had caught the Manhattan bug. When the cricket season ended in England in September, I went back as soon as I could, arriving just in time to watch the Yankees' legendary World Series 'sweep'. The victorious Yankees were treated to an orgy of kitsch celebrations. When I stumbled into the ticker-tape parade, I began to understand how seriously the Americans take their 'good ol' ball game'. It would have made even the vainest Roman emperor blush.

Baseball was everywhere. So many DJs were asking fans to call in with their personal tributes to the Yankee heroes that the radio seemed to be tuned to Yankees FM at every frequency. Getting into a cab, the recorded voice of the Yankees manager Joe Torre beseeched me to 'buckle up for safety'. Every other person I passed in the street appeared to be wearing specially printed 'Yanks Are the Champs' T-shirts. Others brandished broomsticks to emphasise the 4-0 'sweep'.

I was finding out the way they 'did' sporting success in America. The champs are certainly made to feel like champs. When the dreams of American athletes come true, reality can scarcely be any less vivid and exuberant than in their wildest adolescent sporting fantasies. In a winner-take-all society, being on the right side of the line must feel quite something.

My next extended trip to New York was even more fortuitously timed. There's only one thing New Yorkers love more than one of their baseball clubs being in the World Series: it is when both of their teams, the Yankees and the Mets, are competing for what they consider to be the title of World Champions. That was the situation in the autumn of 2000 when I arrived in Manhattan with the half-formed idea that I

wanted to write a book about baseball and cricket. The baseball frenzy I witnessed made up my mind about the project.

They even have a special name for an all-New York World
Series: a Subway Series. You can watch all the live sport in the
world that really matters just by taking the Number 7 or the
Number 11 to Shea Stadium or Yankee Stadium.

A Subway Series! The magic those words conveyed. The
very phrase evoked the 1950s – baseball's golden era, an age
of innocence, of legends, an age of baseball supremacy. That
was what baseball needed, some magic from the 1950s –
when the dynastic Yankees battled the upstart Brooklyn
Dodgers; when not only fans but the players travelled to the
games by subway; when the *New York Times* not only edited
but printed its newspapers in Gotham's Midtown; when pho-
tographs were in black and white but memories were
indelible; when baseball was king among sports and New
York ruled baseball.

Between 1936 and 1956 there were ten Subway Series, and
seven from 1947 to 1956. It was a good time to be a baseball
fan in New York. But then nothing: a forty-four year hiatus,
during which time, heaven forbid, other cities got their hands
on the World Series silverware.

How New York made up for those lost years. The parades
and broomsticks of 1998, I would quickly find out, would be
nothing compared to Subway Series baseball fever. The New
York papers, usually thick even on quiet news days, were
now bursting with extra pull-out, fold-out and pin-up sections devoted to every conceivable facet of baseball – the
history of New York baseball, the evolution of the Subway
Series, the clash of the managers, the key head-to-head player

battles, the rivalry between the stars' supermodel girlfriends. Discovering who had the edge in every department became an epic challenge. A Yankee might be dating Miss World, but the Mets catcher was going out with the *Playboy* Playmate of the Millennium! 'Let's Get Ready to Rumble!' the front pages roared, 'It's Showtime!'

Mayor Rudolph W. Giuliani, conservatism's hard man and a lifelong Yankee fan, joined the frenzy. Two days before the series began, he ended a speech about a new cancer project by saying, 'Now I'm going back to think about the Yankees, because that's all I can think about today.' The next day, he devoted twenty minutes of a thirty-minute news conference to the Yankees. It is difficult to imagine London's Ken Livingstone, whose office is considerably less powerful than Mr Giuliani's, so openly putting his private sporting affiliations at the top of his agenda.

Sport was so dominant that it was easy to forget that there was also a presidential election around the corner. Election? What election? In its last edition before the presidential election, the *New York Observer*, playing on the title of Roger Kahn's epic baseball book *The Boys of Summer*, led with the headline: 'Bush and Gore: The Boys of Bummer.' It struck a chord. Many New Yorkers did prefer to contemplate their own two baseball teams competing for the World Series rather than watch two Southerners fight it out for the presidency. As movie director Nora Ephron put it, 'We got a chance to say what we all secretly believe – that we don't need anyone at all in the rest of the country, even to play baseball.'

I had walked into the most talked about sporting event in

New York's recent history. I could scarcely believe my luck. Even baseball atheists were getting caught up in the city's celebration of its own World Series. If you hadn't enjoyed it at first, before long so many people told you that they were loving it, and that *you* had to be loving it too, that you got swept along on a tide of communal enthusiasm.

As for me, even though I was really only a visitor in the most fluid society on earth, I was feeling a strange, generalised sense of community. I was beginning to feel *part* of something! Was this really a special moment? Had Gotham come together? Or had my bullshit detector been switched off?

If the theatre and extravagance of baseball were new to me, in many other respects I recognised the game as cricket's bastard son. For a start, both games are fundamentally a duel. A cricket coach used to tell me to look at the bowler before every ball and say to myself: 'This ball is a contest between me and you, and I'm going to win it.' Baseball is the same. Every pitch is a direct contest between the pitcher and the batter – a battle of wills and skills. In the final reckoning, no amount of support or teamwork can actually throw the ball for the pitcher or hit the ball for the batter. As with cricket, it is a team game played by individuals with a collective goal.

But the duels in baseball and cricket – unlike the boxing match or the rugby front row – are somewhat abstracted. It is possible to win it without appearing to be overtly pugilistic. At some level you need to be a fighter to succeed in either baseball or cricket; but not necessarily obviously so. Both games take all sorts – from quiet, reflective types to up-and-at-'em aggressors.

They are both slow, fluid games – criticised by non-believers for being boring – with plenty of in-built pauses for the players and spectators to think about the next moment of confrontation. Rather than breathless, non-stop games, they are 'what do you think will happen next?' sports. Both baseball and cricket grow on you, seduce you, absorb you. 'A good football match is a good film,' as Simon Barnes of *The Times* put it, 'a good Test series is a great novel – that is to say, it becomes something you live with.'

The past, too, is omnipresent in both sports. Of all games, cricket and baseball have been most preoccupied with their 'golden ages', and a sense of lost innocence or perceived betrayal of the past. That history so informs the two games deepens their appeal; but at times their obsession with the past may have led them to neglect the present and the future. Their public images have certainly always been conservative.

They have also both inspired more than their fair share of writers, a testament to their reputations as high-minded and heavyweight sports somehow removed from the mass of undifferentiated sporting experience. There is lots of good cricket writing, from the West Indian C. L. R. James's Marxist theories to Alan Ross's elegant perceptions, and still more, as I would discover, about baseball.

Baseball also has the same multisensory mystic appeal as cricket. The crisp crack of the ash bat on baseball hide is one of baseball's great talking points, just as cricket fans eulogise about the calming sound of willow on leather. 'I'd wake up with the smell of the ballpark in my nose and the cool of the grass in my feet,' W. P. Kinsella wrote in his novel *Shoeless Joe*, 'the thrill of the grass.' I, too, as a cricketer, wake up with that feeling. Even now, when I play so much, I haven't lost that boyish excitement so many of us felt as children when we smelt the grass being cut for the first time in spring.

I would, I'm sure, have been a baseball player – at some level – if I had been born in America. I sensed that from the first few pitches I saw and the first lines I read about the game. It is cricket's spiritual cousin. Before I even went to a major league ballgame, I was seduced by baseball's rich culture: the literature, the precision and relentless scrutiny of baseball statistics, the quirky articulateness of the commentary, and above all the extraordinary devotion that baseball inspires among all different types of Americans, from philosophy professors to bartenders. It is a connoisseur's game for everyone.

Though most cricket fans would probably immediately appreciate that ambience, they might not pick up baseball's rules quite so easily. Cricket is notoriously difficult to explain, and I am only marginally more confident about clarifying the rules of baseball to the Brits.

The equivalent of the wicket is the 'strike zone', an imaginary area directly over the batting plate, between the height of batter's knees and his chest. The batter stands alongside the plate, and usually tries to hit pitches thrown into the strike zone, and, if he is sufficiently disciplined, seeks to leave those which miss the strike zone (known as 'balls'). The batter has three 'strikes'.

If a batter receives four 'balls' (balls that aren't in the strike zone and therefore unhittable) before he has conceded three strikes or hits in the air to a fielder, he is allowed to 'walk' to first base – a fourth of the way towards his team scoring a run. So the score immediately relevant to the head-to-head battle between the pitcher and the batter is expressed as the number of balls relative to the number of strikes. Scores of 1-0, 2-0, 2-1, 3-0 and 3-1 (pronounced one-and-oh, two-and-oh) mean the batter is happy and the pressure is on the pitcher. 0-1, 0-2, 1-1 and 1-2 mean the pitcher is ahead. 3-2 is a 'full count' – and one error either way will decide the issue.

But the pitcher doesn't want to throw into the middle of the strike zone. That is what the batter is looking for: a 'hanger' right in his hitting arc. He wants to pitch into the outer edges of the strike zone – inside, outside, high, low – where it is difficult for the batter to make contact. The umpire's interpretation of what constitutes the strike zone varies between the American and National Leagues and from umpire to umpire. It is of the utmost importance. It determines what the pitcher can get away with. All of which makes baseball a game of strategy as much as instinct; as Roger Kahn put it, it is 'chess at ninety miles an hour'.

That is the hardest part to understand. The rest is more obvious and relatively analogous with cricket. There are three outs (wickets) per inning, but nine innings in all – so there is a total of twenty-seven outs in all, rather than the twenty wickets in a two-innings cricket match. But rather than four or five days, a baseball match only takes about three hours (it always finishes on the day it begins), proof of how much easier baseball outs are to come by than cricketing wickets. (There has to be a winner and a loser, of course.

Try explaining to Americans that some five-day cricket matches end in a *draw* . . .)

Outs are two-a-penny in baseball; but runs are like gold dust, as typical scores like 1-3, 4-0, 5-3 demonstrate. Soccer goals probably constitute the highest valued currency in the world of sport, but baseball runs are not far behind.

That means batting, or 'offense' as it is called, must be pretty difficult. And it is. The best batters in the League only hit .300, the benchmark of absolute quality. That does not mean they hit .300 of the pitches they receive, which would be superhuman. It means they have a .300 likelihood of hitting safely (without being caught or thrown out at a base) in their entire 'at-bat' – what a cricket batsman would call one innings. One run, three times in ten! Hitting .300 means you fail seven-tenths of the time, and that's if you're one of the best. Imagine *that* prospect hanging over you as you get out of bed and go to work each morning.

As a batsman in cricket, the difficulties of baseball hitting immediately caught my attention. But if failure is that common and inevitable, I worked out that it had to be less traumatic. In baseball you might fail 70 per cent of the time, but you have more 'lives' (because you are allowed three strikes) in an 'at-bat', more 'at-bats' in a game, and more games in a week. In cricket, where you are expected to get thirty or forty on an average day, you have only one life – as any batsman will morbidly explain. During a series against the West Indies, Mike Brearley referred to the bench where the next batsman sat as 'the condemned chair'.

The odds might be heavily in favour of the cricket batsman surviving this ball, or this over – but the guillotine of dismissal always hangs over us. One mistake, one unplayable ball, one bad decision, and our day is probably ruined and possibly completely over. Baseball's .300 looks a bit rosier when you think about that.

The equivalent of the cricket batsman, then, is not the hitter but the pitcher. He lives in fear of conceding a run, of blotting his copybook, letting the side down. He is more likely to be hit if he pitches badly, but he might also throw the perfect pitch only to see a man mountain of creatine-enhanced muscle launch it into the back row. Then he has nowhere to hide; the rest of his team-mates on the field are all primarily hitters first, fielders second, and none of them pitchers. Now we all have to get a run ourselves, just to get even, they are thinking, and we all know how difficult *that* is, don't we! You have done this to us. You and you alone.

Even if his team-mates have no such thoughts, it is easy for the pitcher to slip into that paranoid mentality. Every head that goes down in the outfield is an implicit attack on his failings. Poor old pitcher.

For the first time in my life I was beginning to feel sorry for the guys who start with the ball, and try to deliver it as fast as they can, rather than the guys who, like me, try to hit it.

Quite apart from having to decide if I preferred pitchers to hitters, I inevitably considered whether I would enjoy the life of a major league baseballer. I'd enjoy the money, for certain. The New York Mets' *minimum* salary is $200,000 a year. You can buy a lot of good cricketers for $200,000.

But there is a price to pay, and it comes in the form of relentless media scrutiny. The New York media, in particular, expects only the best from its ballplayers. The merest slip in performance will be talked to death on every all-night radio phone-in, and turned into a hundred graphics in the following day's papers. The culture of American sport is as unforgiving of failure as it is extravagant in its praise of success.

County cricketers, in comparison, get neither the cash nor the ticker-tape parades; but nor do they have to deal with the relentless glare of media attention. More often than not, even after a thrilling Sunday League match, they can slink off into the night without hearing their shortcomings discussed on the radio all the way home.

So how would I feel, as a sportsman unused to that level of critical scrutiny, if the zoom lens were suddenly pointed at me? I hope one day it will be.

And the second big question in my mind? Would I actually be any good at this baseball business?

2

THE SUBWAY SERIES, NEW YORK, OCTOBER 2000

By the time the World Series started I had become a fully signed up Mets fan, for partly noble, partly cynical reasons. The nobility came in the form of the familiar English habit of supporting the underdog. The Yankees had not only won the last two World Series, they were also a world famous sporting franchise. They are baseball's aristocrats.

The Mets are a relatively new franchise compared to the Yankees. When the much-loved Brooklyn Dodgers relocated to California in 1957, becoming the Los Angeles Dodgers overnight, the Mets filled the baseball vacuum left in New York. The Dodgers had always had a blue-collar following in comparison to the Yankees, and the Mets inherited some of that underdog spirit. The Yankees, like Manchester United, have legions of foreign fans (and plenty who don't live in New York). They scarcely need any more. So I deduced that supporting the Mets was the only discerning and honourable choice.

The second, more pressing reason to follow the Mets emerged during a chance conversation at a friend's birthday party in Massachusetts. When I explained to a fellow guest about my plan to write a comparison of cricket and baseball, she offered to introduce me to her friend, Nelson Doubleday, who co-owns the Mets franchise. That was a 'no-brainer', as managers say. And I guessed it might not be tactful to turn up at the Doubleday house and say, 'Wasn't it great that the Yankees won the World Series all over again!'

In the shorter term, I looked into buying tickets for the Subway Series. The black market was my only chance, where $1500 would buy me a moderately good seat for one of the games. 'Bite the bullet and buy one,' a friend suggested, 'for the history of it, you know.' I was lukewarm about history at that price.

But even from the living-room armchair rather than ringside seat, the hyped-up opening game didn't disappoint. 'All tied up' until the twelfth innings, the third phase of 'extra innings play', Jose Vizcaino – who rarely made it into the Yankees starting line-up – finally settled the issue with a two-out bases-loaded single to leftfield.

Game 2, aside from being the second game of the most hotly anticipated World Series in years, had extra special baggage. It was the grudge game, the rematch between Yankee pitcher Roger Clemens and Mets star hitter Mike Piazza. During the 'regular season' Mets–Yankees game, the scowling, straight-shooting, hard-throwing Clemens had 'beaned' Piazza with a vicious 'inside' head-high fast ball that thudded on to Piazza's helmet at about 97 m.p.h. Piazza retired concussed; Clemens didn't apologise; many thought it was deliberate –

Playing Hard Ball

and baseball, of course, unlike cricket, prohibits intentional head-high pitching.

Yankees manager Joe Torre tried to calm everything down the day before Game 2. 'I'd like to believe,' he suggested diplomatically, 'that the fans would rather watch the World Series than to see if Roger Clemens is going to hit him again, or if Mike is going to throw the bat at him.' As it developed on the night, Torre had it the wrong way round. In Piazza's first at-bat against Clemens, his bat shattered on contact with a fast ball. When the barrel of the bat, about two pounds of splintered but solid wood, landed near the pitching mound, Clemens promptly picked it up and hurled it at Piazza, who was jogging casually towards first base. It missed him by a few inches. But in true baseball spirit, both dugouts emptied into a mass confrontation, where, despite considerable hectoring and gesturing, no one actually threw a punch. 'I thought it was the ball,' Clemens helpfully explained.

The game was now subsidiary to the Rog-goes-batty incident. The handling of the mini-drama was a classic example of the evolving American news story. Even when it isn't actually evolving any more, you just keep repeating the story so far. The TV producers played it, replayed it, replayed it in reverse angle, queried the motivation behind it, counter-queried the motivation, imagined the reaction, challenged that imagined reaction, then went back to the first replay to see if it had become more conclusive with the passing of time. It hadn't – so they tried to reverse angle again. Within half an hour I'd seen the batty-bat-hurl so many times I knew which way the splinters on Piazza's shattered bat were pointing.

Feeling battered by the replays of the incident, and with the Yankees seemingly out of sight at 6-0 going into the last inning, I decided against watching the last rites and headed off to my girlfriend's place in the Lower East Side of Manhattan. The short walk from East 9th Street to Suffolk Street – past the body-piercing parlours and leather shops of the East Village, then the converted lofts of NoHo, and finally through the once infamous but now ultra-cool Alphabet City – only takes about twenty minutes, the typical length of one full inning of a baseball game. By the time I got there, the Yankees would have won, and I wouldn't have to suffer any more – though I knew that I wouldn't be able to resist checking the final score in the deli across the street.

About halfway, when I was crossing Avenue A just north of Houston Street, huge cheers erupted from three bars on the other side of the road. More Mets strikeouts, surely, more Clemens victims, more Yankee bullying. But it wasn't the cocksure cheer of fans already certain of victory, a 'let's really savour this, lads, because we're home and hosed' sort of cheer. It was an ecstatic, surprised, elated noise – like the cheers from supporters of minor footballing nations when their boys knock one in against Brazil in a World Cup game. They weren't cheering victory: they were cheering the *chance* of victory, and the survival of their dreams. So it had to be runs for the Mets.

And it was. I stopped outside the window of Ed's Bar on Houston, and just in time to see the replay of Piazza – *Piazza! Justice!* – hitting one of his improbable home runs. Let it be off Clemens, I thought, let it be off Clemens! It wasn't; sadly, it was hit off Rivera.

In true American style, Ed's Bar was neither a Mets joint nor a Yankees stronghold. Unlike English football fans, American sports fans don't seem to think that watching a game with opposition fans spoils the occasion. In fact, they seem to like the diversity. It's not unusual to see two friends walk to the same game wearing different baseball strips. And in Ed's Bar, alongside little pockets of flag-waving Mets or Yankees fans, I could see several couples sitting together who were supporting different teams.

There's nothing better than when a dead game suddenly comes to life, when despair turns to hope. I remember watching a Kent Sunday League game in the late 1980s against Hampshire, one of those John Player League specials that finished in almost complete darkness. Not one person in the ground believed Kent had a chance of winning. We were eight wickets down, and needed a hundred runs off the last ten overs. Not even a fantasist like me thought we had a chance. Dad, a more experienced fan, was already packing up our stuff and moving towards the car park.

'One more over!' I begged him. It was lucky we stayed. The Kent all-rounder Richard Ellison – a former pupil of my dad's – came good that over. He hit two sixes just over our Ford Sierra; we didn't move a muscle for the rest of the game for fear of breaking our good fortune, and Kent won the game. It was one of my best ever days as a fan.

The next few minutes in New York looked like being a repeat of that day in Canterbury. Thanks to Piazza's home run, the Mets had closed to 6-3. But two Mets batters were out, so to win outright they had to score four runs before losing their third batter. Very unlikely, but the momentum was with them. When Jay Payton hit home run number two inside five minutes, with a man on base as well, the Mets were 5-6 and closing fast.

I was still cursing myself for having given up on the Mets earlier in the night while writing tomorrow's headlines in my head. 'Miracle Mets' indeed. Surely, after all that, they'd finish off this recovery with a win? What a great time to be writing a book about them! At which point Rivera 'found his good stuff', as they say in baseball. Strike one was quickly followed by strike two – still one life left, boys, remember Botham at Headingley, remember Ellison at Canterbury, come on, don't quit on me now – which was rapidly succeeded by strike three. Lights out. Yankees win. Another one in the eye for my eternal optimism.

I resumed my walk back to the Lower East Side – properly down now, having had my hopes rekindled, only to be cruelly extinguished. A stranger stopped me as I waited to cross Ludlow Street.

'Did the Mets get up?'

'No.'

'Did Piazza score?'

'Yes.'

Sudden elation in the stranger's voice – 'Off Clemens? Off Clemens?'

'No.'

Even on nights as dramatic as Game 2, I couldn't completely lose myself as a straightforward baseball fan. I was a fan, but a fan who couldn't quite forget that he was a professional practitioner of another sporting discipline.

For most people one of the joys of watching sport is the escapism it offers. For that day, or for those ninety minutes, or those three hours, you can forget your homework, or the politics in the office, or the argument you've just had with your girlfriend. It is an innocent and alternative world, to which you can cheaply and comfortably travel just by switching on your television.

Watching sport also affords endless potential for wish-fulfilment fantasies. That will be me one day, we all used to think, scoring the match-winning penalty in front of 50,000 cheering fans. And even for the people who realise it never will be them, there are always the might-have-beens. 'If only my mother hadn't made me take up the piano,' they say to themselves, 'I would have been the footballer I always could have been – I had trials for Arsenal juniors, you know, when I was eight.'

The fan/player equation changes somewhat when you are a professional sportsman. It is no longer what you could have been, but what you are. And yet you do your job – play sport – with the same number of imperfections and inadequacies as everyone else does theirs. You know how easy sport looks on TV, because you have watched it, and you know how hard it is in real life, because you have played it. Where most fans are thinking, 'how glamorous it must be', you wonder, 'how would I cope?' or even, 'how did I cope?' You might still desperately look forward to being in the spotlight. But you have lost the innocence of the armchair fan. And there is no going back.

When I used to watch Kent at Canterbury as a young boy, I considered it a certainty that one day I would *play* for them.

What I never considered was that I might *fail* for them. Of course you cannot sustain that level of confidence, as any batsman will tell you, all that far into your adult career.

Even when I watched Test cricket, which between the ages of six and thirteen I did almost every day it was on television, I used to wonder why batsmen got out playing bad shots. Couldn't he see all those slip fielders Malcolm Marshall had put there just for that shot? 'He's a pretty good bowler, Ed,' my dad would explain.

How quickly things change. As an eighteen-year-old playing my second first-class match, I remember swishing almost involuntarily at one of the first balls I faced from Devon Malcolm. 'What on earth was that?' I wondered. A terrible shot was the answer.

And once you have been in that situation yourself, you cannot help holding back when you watch someone else make the same mistake. You haven't gone soft and apologetic – you still recognise it as an error, and appreciate it as such. You are probably just less inclined to shout off about it.

Even when I watch a sport other than cricket – which demands skills quite different from my own – I sometimes transpose its psychological challenges into my own realm of experience. Want to take the last penalty in the shoot-out to win the World Cup? Easy. Want to be underneath a sky-er that is lost in the lights at the Melbourne Cricket Ground to win the World Cup? Even if the answer is yes, understanding the skill probably makes you pause for a second.

Those mixed emotions of the player/fan recurred to me during the Subway Series. I was a rapt observer, enjoying the ambience of a new game and a new sporting culture, but I was also a professional from a different code, whose job demands similar challenges, and I inevitably wondered how I would front up.

As a player, you also become more irritable about familiar sporting clichés. I was often riled during the Subway Series when I heard people talking loosely about 'losing concentration'. I probably used to talk like that myself. It is the easiest criticism of all. 'He lost concentration on that four-foot putt,' people say, as though it's like forgetting to lock your car door. Just a lack of attention. Sometimes it is, but how much more often is failure the result of trying too hard, of tensing up, of overrevving? That is much more often the cause, I think, than underrevving. Most sportsmen try too hard, not too little. Of course, if you interpret concentration as the absence of irrelevant thought, which it probably is, then most errors do come down to a loss of concentration. But I doubt most people use it in that sense. They use concentration to mean attention. It's a classic lounge room cliché.

The 'bottler' (or 'choker') chat got me going too. It cropped up during the Subway Series concerning Mike Piazza. Coming into the World Series, Piazza had a lifetime batting average of over .300, an astonishing record in the modern game. But in his limited experience of post-season play, where the games tend to count for more, his hit production had dipped. 'Mike can't step up,' the papers repeated *ad nauseam*. In principle, I'm not at all against that kind of comparative statistic or that type of judgement – the players understand the pressure and the scrutiny when they sign on the dotted line.

But the difficulty comes in judging at what point the

statistic and the judgement *mean* anything. When does a one-off failure become a sequence? When does a sequence become a trend, a trend a body of evidence? When is a body of evidence more than enough to know that he will 'never do it'? They are all difficult judgements that selectors and coaches have to make all the time. Leaping to the final conclusion at the first opportunity isn't being a 'thinking fan'; it is not being bothered to think. In Piazza's case, incidentally, it was a trend, but not a meaningful one. He had a great post-season in 2000.

Sometimes sportsmen do bottle it, and there is no running away from it. Occasionally, they even admit it. But other times, they are simply beaten by someone else. I remember watching the play-offs for a major American golf tournament. Both men played very well. Neither looked nervous; one of them lost, the other won. The next morning, I heard someone say about the loser, 'He's a fucking bottling bottler with no bottle, that bloke.' Aside from wondering how many variations of the word 'bottle' you could use in one sentence – he had managed two nouns and one adjective so far – my first thought was, 'And who the fuck are you?'

Silly as it may sound coming from a twenty-four-year-old, watching the Subway Series also made me think about the brevity of a sportsman's career. That is probably why sportsmen are atypically aware of the passing years. All through childhood I sought to emulate people who had achieved success very young: David Rocastle, dead at a tragically early age, who played for Arsenal at seventeen and England at twenty; Mike Atherton, who played for England at twenty-one and scored a Test hundred at twenty-two; Jonathan

Davies, who by his early twenties was already one of the best rugby players in the world.

Like lots of sportsmen, I too got off to a good start – albeit nothing approaching the achievements of those mentioned above. Then suddenly a year or two later, you seem to be watching a whole batch of brilliant sportsmen much younger even than you. 'God, that Manchester United midfielder's only nineteen,' you start saying to yourself, 'and he's already a star. I'm nowhere near where I would like to be and I'm pushing *twenty-four* . . .' It's not a serious point, really, and I mention it only mischievously, but it's a funny feeling nonetheless.

So when the Yankees' twenty-five-year-old lead-off hitter Derek Jeter hit Bobby Jones's first Game 4 pitch out of Shea Stadium (home of the Mets) – his twelfth consecutive hit in World Series matches, in his third trip to the World Championships – I joked that I had some serious work to do. Even assuming I managed to break into the World Cup squad for 2003 (and William Hill will give generous odds on that), I would need to play until 2011 to emulate Jeter's feat. But then again, cricket World Cups only come around once every four years!

The Mets, meanwhile, were struggling. The Mets' Ric Reed beat Orlando Hernandez in Game 3, but then Bobby Jones lost to Danny Neagle in Game 4. The bad news was that they were one game away from losing the World Series; the good was that the game was at Shea Stadium; the best news was that – thanks to the sports editor of *The Times* – I had been given a ticket. Finally, I would be able to use the

subway, rather than the remote control, to watch the Subway
Series.

Yankee Stadium, which sits at the southern tip of the
Bronx, not so far into enemy territory as to dissuade the
Manhattan types, is much the more famous of New York's
ball parks. 'The House that Ruth Built', allegedly constructed
on the money raised from soaring gate receipts that followed
the Babe's trade to New York, is thirty years older than Shea,
and widely considered the more homely and atmospheric. I'd
driven past Yankee Stadium scores of times, and marvelled at
the huge lettering on the concrete walls that lists the years in
which the Yankees won the World Series.

But Shea was all new to me, and I felt quite pleased with
myself that I was travelling to Shea for the first time, appropriately enough on the subway 'number 7 train', on the night
that might settle the first Subway Series for forty-four years. It
gave me the same feeling of satisfaction as reading Tom
Wolfe's *Bonfire of the Vanities* – years after everyone had badg-
ered me that 'I had to read it now' – while I sat in Central
Park, only a stone's throw from the Park Avenue apartments
Wolfe describes, during my first trip to New York.

As I filtered up the subway stairs into the autumnal twilight, the first thing I saw was the enormous illuminated
silhouette of Shea Stadium. Even from five hundred yards
away I could discern the *Let's Go Mets* banner. It is a baronial
world, big league American sport. And Shea announced itself
as the Mets' home, their patch, their back yard, at every
opportunity. Even if I hadn't been 'up for' the game (and I
was) the short walk to the stadium would have got me in the
mood.

I was sitting in the first tier of seats in leftfield, just in range for a slightly 'pulled' out-of-bounds near-home run. 'There's nothing to worry about, then,' my host from Major League Baseball told his other guests, 'if Piazza slams one up here, at least we've got a professional athlete to catch it!' That's bound to happen now, I said to myself . . .

An employee from Major League Baseball mentioned that 'Tom and Nicole' (before the split, but long after they had ceased to need surnames) had turned up as expected, and that the cameras had been given their seat numbers in order to pick them out. The film studios' PR people inform the baseball PR people, who inform the TV people – and everyone wins on the publicity plugs.

Meanwhile, as I stared at the huge slice of deep green grass in front of me, two questions came to mind. First, how does anyone hit a ball from home plate to the outfield fence? It looked an awfully long way – I would later find out, when I stood in the batter's box, that it *is* an awfully long way. Secondly, how does anyone throw a ball from the deep outfield all the way to home plate? It's hard enough when the ropes are deep at the Oval (which they rarely are these days). It looked as though, in cricketing parlance, you could run seven if you managed to get it to the outfield extremities. It says a great deal about the quality of the throwing that it is so difficult just to get on to third base in one hit.

After the *de rigueur* singing of the national anthem – only one is required in this 'world' final – the players were extravagantly introduced on the very loud loudspeaker. Their fanfare entries into the arena were accompanied not only by a roar from the crowd, but a short excerpt from a rock or rap song, a leitmotif for each competitor. Cricketers get the same treatment now, if not at the same volume, during day-night games.

What we never get, so far as I am aware, is a simultaneous sequence of cartoon images that illustrates an aspect of the player's name or personality. The name-image is played on the giant scoreboard – which is about the size of what cricketers would consider a grandstand.

So the Mets pitcher Al Leiter, whose job is to strike out Yankee batters, is introduced on the scoreboard with a demonstration of someone turning off a light: 'LEIT OUT', it explains. To introduce the Hawaiian outfielder Benny Agbayani, who wears fifty on his shirt to commemorate his home state, the fiftieth of the union, our choreographed scoreboard amorphously mutates into a picture of a pina colada, accompanied by the question: 'HOW ABOUT SOME HAWAIIAN PUNCH?'

In case that thought has made you a little thirsty, a drinks vendor shouting 'beer here!' comes right to your seat, asks if you want a Coke, orangeade or Budweiser (the airship *Bud 1*, meanwhile, is circling above the stadium to help you with your choice). Another salesman is quickly on hand offering 'sizzling hot dogs, warm pretzels, iced Ben and Jerry's all-natural Vermont ice-cream'. This can't go on all night, can it? The man next to me explains that it can – every twenty minutes or so, in fact.

Beside the main scoreboard is another, much smaller electronic screen. +17.5 . . . it told me, then –5 . . . +16.5 . . . Uh? I thought we hadn't started yet? In fact, it is not the baseball score at all, but another equally important set of results: the

Nasdaq stockmarket score. A man next to me in a Mets cap sighs: 'Damned things are down again; I should have got rid of them months ago.' In case they're bored before the baseball has even begun, or faced with a minute of unwanted introspection, fans can fill quiet moments in the ball park with eating, drinking, and share-checking.

Then suddenly, almost by accident, I look down at the playing area for the first time in quite a while, and, much to my surprise, there is a ballgame going on. How could I have missed the start? I only eyed up the hot dogs for a second, and studied the scoreboard for a minute, and . . . what? He's out? One out already, and I'm still munching on my frankfurter. The game really is under way. But the theatre, perhaps just as important, has been in full swing for some time.

Sometimes they use giant catapults to fire hot dogs into the crowd. Catch it and you can eat it. Lucky you. Even in a minor league ground, when I subsequently watched the Mets in Port St Lucie, rolled up Mets T-shirts were fired into the crowd during 'the seventh inning stretch'. And when a ball was hit out of the stadium, the Tannoy played a loud recording of a window being smashed, 'Could it be your car?' being the implication. Everyone laughed. In the elaborate theatre of American sport, they try to prevent your concentration from slipping. Like radio stations, they work on the theory that, once you've switched off, you're lost for the rest of the day.

In the age of day-night games and coloured clothing, cricket has moved somewhat in that direction. And with considerable success: our day-night game against Surrey at Canterbury in 2001 was a full house and a great day, but I am not sure everyone is ready for a quantum leap into the brash and the brassy. If someone fired a hot dog at a cricket fan like my father while he watched a Kent Championship match, it might ruin his day. It could knock over his flask of tea, or land on Philip Larkin's collected poems.

Cricket's period of transition, as the old has rubbed shoulders with the new, has thrown up some classic moments. During one of the first English day-night games at the Oval in 1999, the late Lord Cowdrey was introduced to Surrey's furry 'Lion' mascot. 'The Lion didn't look terribly interested, I have to say,' he said mischievously afterwards. 'In fact, I thought the Lion had it about right.'

English sport has long been playing commercial catch-up. The first major league baseball match to be played under lights took place on 24 May 1935, when the general manager of the Cincinnati Reds arranged for President Roosevelt to push a button in the White House that lit up Crosley Field in Cincinnati. It wasn't until the 1970s that Kerry Packer's World Series Cricket followed suit. And it was only three years ago that county teams were given American-style pseudonyms, like Yorkshire Phoenix, Surrey Lions, Kent Spitfires.

It is a big question facing English sport: how American should we become? Should we back our product, the sporting action itself, to stand up to the competition from new forms of entertainment, and hope to retain the core supporters? Or do everything we can to modernise and jazz up our sport in an attempt to attract new young fans? The implied question being: do English sports fans have the same innate love of razzmatazz as Americans, which is currently being undernourished, or are they qualitatively different in wanting just to turn up and watch a game of sport?

Playing Hard Ball

It is not an issue that seems ever to have troubled baseball. In reply to the question 'How American should we be?' the answer is always a resounding 'VERY AMERICAN'. The routines of the game have become laden with patriotic meaning. In the 1900s, so the story goes, an extremely fat baseball fan, finding his seat at the ball park confining, heaved himself to his feet to stretch during the seventh inning. Because the three hundred pound man was President William Howard Taft, everyone around him stood up respectfully. Ever since, all baseball games have had an official 'seventh inning stretch'. In Game 5 at Shea Stadium, it took me a while to work out what was going on. 'Will you all rise please,' the Tannoy boomed, 'for a rendering of "Take Me Out to the Ball Game".' The famous fairground tune began, a ditty that has so much American resonance, and amazingly, everyone stood up. In England, only the Queen would induce such dutiful behaviour.

I had no desire to stand up, but, against my expectations, went along with the mass of conformity, stood up and started singing, 'Take me out to the ball game . . .' What was happening to me? I would never have done it in England. It was like being an agnostic who had wandered into an Italian town, stumbled upon a Catholic procession and ended up carrying a crucifix.

When I wasn't standing up and singing, I was trying to keep up with the scoreboard, which displayed enough information to keep the fastest shorthand wizard writing at top speed. Even this longhand slowcoach was running out of space on his match programme. The scoreboard provides details of every out, every run batted in, every fielding error.

And the statistical orgy isn't limited only to the game in hand: sometimes a player's career figures flash up, or his career post-season stats, and his figures in this World Series – and so on, *ad infinitum*.

Statistics are the stuff of baseball, its crystalline essence. But baseball is generating statistics faster than anyone can master them. Aside from recording the score, the role of the scoreboard is to come up with bite-sized stats that are as easy to swallow as a mouthful of the special World Series beer. Who's doing well? Who's on a streak? Who's hot and who's not? But in doing so, they don't shy away from pointing out the other type of statistics, the statistics of failure – no matter to whom they belong.

At least one man on the field that night, the Yankees centre fielder and all-star batter Bernie Williams, is sick of hearing about statistics. At thirty-one, he is one of the biggest names in the sport, with a batting average of nearly .300. Two years ago he signed one of the biggest contracts in baseball at the time, earning Bernie take-home pay of around $11 million a year. That's Mickey Mouse money in today's market, in which Alex Rodriguez is guaranteed to earn not less than $20 million every year for the next ten years. But Williams, though he might be unassuming and unflashy, is a serious star.

But there's been a hiccup, a recurring fault. He can't score a run in the World Series – and this is his fourth World Series with the Yankees. I don't mean that in the metaphorical sense of 'can't score as many runs as usual'. I mean: *not one run*. In twenty-two at-bats going into this game, he hasn't even scored a single, let alone a home run. This chink in his armour has been exhaustively analysed in every newspaper, sports radio phone-in, and living room in America. Why can't Bernie hit on the biggest stage of all? 'He gets paid all this money,' everyone is saying, 'and he can't even make contact with the ball in the World Series. What *is* going on?'

While Bernie Williams was standing 'on deck', next in line to bat in Game 5 at Shea – which, if you're a New Yorker, is possibly the biggest baseball game for forty-four years – he might just have caught a glimpse of that giant 'Leits Out, Hawaiian Punch' scoreboard. 'BERNIE WILLIAMS', it would have told him in massive capitals, 'HAS NOT SCORED A RUN IN 22 WORLD SERIES AT-BATS.' Just in case he'd forgotten.

Maybe he didn't look at it. He may have been too deeply in his 'bubble' or in the 'zone', as the sports psychologists say, to notice any distractions. As an experienced major leaguer, he's certainly used to it all. And because of his perpetually calm body language, we'll never know if it affected him at all. In fact, it is beside the point. What was so compelling from my point of view, as someone from a different sporting culture, was observing the relentlessly public nature of American sporting analysis. There is no escaping it. Top-flight American sport is not a good place to find yourself if you don't like criticism – accurate, inarguable, factually supported, nail-on-the-head-now-prove-me-wrong criticism. In a winner-takes-all society, anyone who loses should expect the worst.

Back in Game 5, a do-or-die tie for the Mets, the Yankees were up again, 4-2 this time, in the ninth and final inning. So the Mets had three at-bats, at the very least, to save themselves by scoring two runs. Everyone in the crowd was making the same calculation: who were the next batters due up? (In baseball, where only three outs are required to end an inning, the batting order does not start again with each inning. So if batter number seven was third out in the last inning, batter eight goes in first next time, and so on.) It's . . . yes . . . it's . . . it's PIAZZA! It could all be down to him. Here was divine intervention: the best power hitter in the Mets team – and a man with many scores to settle – might come in to bat when it really counted, to keep the series alive.

It all went according to the script. The Mets managed to get one batter on first base (so any subsequent home run would be worth two runs, and level the score at 4-4), while suffering two 'outs'. So the equation for Piazza, who was next to bat, was simple: hit a home run and tie up the game; fail to hit a home run and it's probably 'Leits Out' for good. He hit his second pitch well, high and hard, and for a split second the whole of Shea Stadium contemplated the beauty of sport. My God, we all thought, he's done it. Yankees manager Joe Torre even shouted 'Nooo!'.

But the trajectory of the ball dipped, and it landed safely in the glove of Bernie Williams thirty yards in from the home run wall. Piazza out, Yankees win, series over, no 'Miracle Mets' fairy tale.

My host from Major League Baseball turned to me: 'Do you realise in that second, in one losing hit, Piazza just earned nearly as much as you get for playing a whole season of county cricket?' A sobering thought, but one that probably wouldn't have made Piazza feel any better just then.

As for Bernie Williams, aside from that closing play, his

main role in the drama came earlier in the night. In the second inning, he hit an Al Leiter pitch several rows into the stands for a home run that gave the Yankees a lead they never relinquished – finally putting the 'Leit Out' on that particular losing streak.

3

SPRING TRAINING, FLORIDA, FEBRUARY 2001

Four months after Joe Torre shouted 'Nooo' in Shea Stadium, and Mike Piazza's fly ball landed inside the Yankee outfielder's glove, I was back visiting the world of major league baseball, this time in the 'Sunshine State' of Florida, having been invited to join the Mets at their 2001 Spring Training camp. I could just about manage to visit them in late February without being late for my own cricket pre-season in early March.

Would the pre-season preparations of a multimillion dollar sporting machine like the Mets bear any relation to Kent's annual limbering up? And, more pressingly, would I be any good at hitting a baseball?

Unlike cricket clubs, baseball teams see no reason to leave the country in preparation for a new season. And why would you? One of the things America has over England is that you can escape winter without leaving the mainland, something the very wealthy take full advantage of by having seasonal properties dotted along the eastern seaboard. Thus they can spend July and August in the summer house in temperate Maine or Cape Cod, spring or autumn in South Carolina, winter in Florida, and any time left over in the mandatory New York apartment. Nice work if you can get it.

Baseball clubs, as you would expect, are also on to the great American migration. Every February most of the major league teams – bringing with them all their coaches and backroom staff and many of their administrators – decamp for 'Spring Training' in Florida. Those that don't go to Florida head off to Arizona. No intercontinental travel, no customs, no vast time-zone adjustments. Just a short flight and then straight into serious baseball practice. The added bonus is that there is a built-in system of warm-up games because everyone else is doing the same thing. Not to mention the weather, the golf courses and the swimming.

So I didn't take long to make up my mind when the Mets' co-owner Nelson Doubleday invited me to stay with him in West Palm Beach and hook up with the Mets' Spring Training camp. As research trips go, it wasn't exactly a war-zone location.

It's all a bit different in the cricket world. Even if we had baseball-style money, which we don't, it would still be considerably more difficult for county cricket teams to organise such orderly pre-seasons. We're the only country in Europe, where it rains a great deal, particularly in spring, that plays top-level cricket. All the other countries that do play are thousands of miles away from us.

Nonetheless, eager to get ahead of rival counties, and conscious of the fact that cricketers in sunnier countries now practise almost all year round, the trend in county cricket is to 'report back' earlier and earlier in the spring. My first pre-season in 1996 started on 1 April; in 1999, we checked in on 8 March. You can, of course, do countless fitness tests and have very thorough team meetings in early March. It's playing cricket that's so difficult.

It's hard to know what the ideal weather is for early pre-season. In 2000, it was very bad, but not bad enough. We stuck it out in Canterbury, through the hail and the sleet, getting outside when we could to 'warm up the hands' with some catching practice (gloveless catching practice, that is, for any baseball readers). In 2001, the weather was even worse, which was great: we conceded defeat and went to South Africa for ten days. So most county cricketers want pre-season either to be warm and sunny (dream on), or else so wet that you have to go abroad. Clarity is all we ask for.

Going away, though, is not a catch-all cure. It's vastly preferable to talking tactics in draughty English changing rooms, but it throws up its own problems. It is all very well playing glorious cover drives 'on the up' on flat wickets and under blue skies in the Southern Hemisphere. It's a bit more difficult when you get home for the season proper and the ball is moving sideways on seaming, green English 'pudding' tracks. If the weather gods are against you, there's no easy way to gear up for the English county season.

In baseball, where the ball doesn't bounce, there is much less variation in the playing conditions. Pitchers have a different feel on the ball when it's warm, and some, like Mike Hampton, hate the cold, but the essential game of baseball remains the same. So because pitchers don't have to run up through muddy outfields, and batters don't have to adjust their swings when it gets chilly, they can move seamlessly from Spring Training to the opening day of the season. March in Florida is all part of the long-established routine of big league baseball.

The Mets are based in Port St Lucie, about thirty miles north of Jupiter Island, a gorgeous 'winter' hideaway for afflu-ent eastern seaboard seasonal commuters. Port St Lucie itself is a largely recent development, part of the relentless subur-banisation of Florida. They describe the ball park as 'quite old', meaning it was built a dozen years ago. There is even talk of building a newer stadium. What would they make, I wonder, of Canterbury's idiosyncratic charm? How would I explain what that old tree is doing on the edge of the outfield?

The pristine-looking concrete ball park, despite being only a minor league ground, is clearly signed from the freeway – rather better, in fact, than many county grounds, some of which have the ability to make me get lost every time I play there. In fact, you can see the home of the Port St Lucie Mets (the name of the minor league team owned by the real New York Mets) from miles around. Nothing could be more different from those county grounds which emerge unex-pectedly at the end of Victorian residential cul-de-sacs, or, like the entrance to Leicester, are hidden in a clearing in a hedge. People mostly find the antique atmosphere of county grounds, the newly pressed scorecards and frayed deck chairs, either charming or anachronistic, usually depending on their more general view of county cricket.

The two-mile drive from the freeway to the ground in Port St Lucie is flanked by large 'Mets Spring Training' banners. Everyone certainly knows about it when the big boys are in town. And even though I arrived on a relatively quiet practice day, long before the start of the season, there was a considerable buzz around the ground. The New York media, the toughest in baseball, was out in force, interviewing players, managers and administrators. Like English football, the baseball hype doesn't die down for long in the off season. Even in February, the *New York Post* and the *Daily News* devote a full page every day to the Mets and Yankees Spring Training. 'Mets First Baseman Has Slight Shoulder Injury', is a typical headline, 'No Throwing for Four Days'.

Out on the field, as the Mets practised for their first warm-up game, there was also plenty of activity. Some were fielding 'fly balls'; others took 'grounders'; batters had batting practice ('BP') in the hitting cages; and pitchers loosened their arms by throwing at catchers. All standard stuff. But there was also a fair amount of indiscernible general movement. This, I have spotted, is an inescapable aspect of pre-seasons. There is never quite enough for everyone to be doing something at all times at pre-season. But the essential thing as a player is never to be seen doing absolutely nothing. As former Yankee pitcher Jim Bouton put it – rather mischievously – in his bestseller, *Ball Four*:

> Another thing you need in Spring Training is a knack for looking busy. There really isn't much to do in Spring Training, and it's a lot like being in the army, where the sergeant will never say anything to you if you *look* like you're doing something. I mean just stopping to tie your shoelace, or walking along briskly as if you have someplace to go.

Privately, I was relieved to see that, although Spring Training was highly efficient, it wasn't so organised as to be unrecognisable from Kent's pre-season. I didn't want to feel amateurish, for God's sake. After all, I was trying to hang on to my 'all very similar apart from the salaries' outlook. But I did have to acknowledge that the Mets had drawn a slightly bigger crowd while they lobbed a ball around than we get for our net sessions. Only a few thousand more, I suppose – slightly more, in fact, than we get for some Championship games. Still, that's easily explained, I consoled myself, by the vast numbers of retired people in Florida with so much time to kill. But on closer inspection, they, well, looked distinctly *young*. Damn.

That afternoon the Mets split into two teams for an inter-squad game. 'In this game, I've got a lot of money on the Mets,' quipped their general manager Steve Philips. I watched from behind the batting plate, surrounded by hundreds of Mets fans trying to get their first glimpse of Mike Piazza. Even the Tannoy was already up and running, announcing the players and referring to one team as 'New York' and the other as 'the Mets'.

Most cricketers find inter-squad games slightly strange. You're playing against your mates, who are often after your place in the team, with no atmosphere and nothing to play for apart from your own progress. You could say experiencing the inevitable fear of failure in those games is excellent practice for the real thing.

One pre-season at Kent, after a month dominated by rain and team talks, the coach demanded that the second team came in to Canterbury on a nominated rest day to bowl at the first-team batsmen. It wasn't a proper game of cricket; just the second team bowlers against the Championship top-order batsmen. It was difficult to work out who was more distraught: the second team at having to come in to field on a freezing April morning, or the first-team batsmen at being told beforehand by the captain that 'selection issues are at stake', and that, in order to imitate match conditions, 'the second team have been instructed to be as aggressive as possible in every way'.

Great. The day before the first game of the season, several of your disgruntled colleagues, all of whom would much rather have the day off as they had been promised, have been given a divine right to abuse you all morning – delaying your two-hour drive through rush-hour traffic to north London, where you were hoping to settle comfortably into the hotel before focusing on the following day's match against Middlesex. Accordingly, the two teams weren't allowed to warm up together or speak to each other before play started. One of the senior batting pros on 'our side' shouted over to the fielding side: 'If you can't get me out, we're all staying here 'til it gets dark! I'm not moving anywhere until you shift me!' 'This is *great*,' the coach said to me from his position as umpire, 'just what you need to get you going for the season!'

I didn't hear too much of all that as 'the Mets' took on 'New York' at Port St Lucie. The rookies looked a bit nervous; the minor leaguers looked eager to please; the stars looked slightly bored. No one pitched for more than one inning, not many fielders stayed out there for the whole game, and none of the big guns was asked to do too much. It was a work out but not a blow out. Todd Zeile was subbed for a minor leaguer while he was on first base – he'd got the hit, now someone else could do the running. Now there's an idea that would go down well among county cricket's senior pros.

I watched the inter-squad game from the ringside seats behind the batting plate, sitting alongside the general manager, the assistant GM and head scout. They quietly took notes on the game, marking down moments where players had surprised them. It was nice to be on the other side of the line for a day – in the stands with a notebook, rather than on the field having notes taken about me. I know only too well that feeling of trying to 'read' the expressions of those who will decide on my place and role in the team. After a while, in fact, you realise it's not even worth bothering.

In case they missed anything, two full-time play-by-play analysts imput every pitch and every swing into a computer-analysis program by pressing an electronic pen against their screen. The flight and 'action' on every pitch is recorded, along with the placement of every hit. 'That takes a lot of the subjectivity out of it,' one coach explained; 'you can help the player to see your opinion for himself.'

The minds behind the Mets focused particularly on the borderline players, who might be invited on to the big league squad roster for the regular season. Unlike in county cricket, where the squad of twenty-five or so players is largely fixed throughout the season, baseball clubs have a steady flow of players coming up from – and going down into – the minor leagues. Being invited to have a chat with the management has very different connotations for those seeking promotion and those fearing demotion. If you're a 'top prospect' you eagerly wait for the phone to ring; if you're a struggling major leaguer, the threat of the minors looms. In *Ball Four*, Jim Bouton refers to being dropped to the minors as 'dying'.

In cricket, being demoted to the second team is bad enough. You could quite easily go from playing at Lord's in a Cup Final to changing in a wooden shed in a second-team game the following week. Accordingly, some players who consider themselves 'first teamers' will go to extraordinary lengths to avoid playing second-team cricket. They try to get into that privileged bracket of 'possibly slightly injured or temporarily out-of-form first-team squad members'. One year, we took a non-playing 'first-team squad member' around the country for half a season as a kind of non-fielding twelfth man. In the ruthless world of baseball, I suspect, he would have been welcomed into the open arms of the minor leagues rather more promptly.

While the senior figures in the club quietly pass preliminary judgement, out on the field the coaches are generally supportive. Even at this early stage, in a game in which the result is meaningless, the batting coach rushed into the dugout to offer a high five to one batter who had just slugged a home run. There is a continual hum of advice and encouragement from the coaching staff to the players – some of it technical and tactical, much of it part of the rhythm of the professional game. When Tiger Woods won the 2001 Masters at Augusta to complete his Grand Slam of Majors, Woods' caddie punched his fist after every good shot – part in congratulation, predominantly in routine affirmation. In baseball, anyone who gets to first base receives a similar tap on the back from the first base coach, who stands immediately next to him, whispering advice, for as long as he stays there.

That is one of the major differences between baseball and cricket, and more generally between American sports and what might loosely be called Commonwealth sports. In America, the flow of coaching advice never stops. In baseball, particularly, if the advice is tactical, the players have little choice in the matter; they do what they are told. A batter might be told not to swing at any pitch, in the hope of earning 'a walk' – so even if his dream pitch is coming towards him, he must control his instinct to hit it. For those of us brought up on the romantic ideal of sporting spontaneity, that seems a little restrictive.

In cricket, on the other hand, along with soccer and rugby, the coach may have great influence before the game starts and during match breaks. But he is consigned to the sidelines for the action of the contest itself. He may or may not exercise his right to shout at his players, but he cannot easily tell them when to pass, hit or kick the ball. Soccer and rugby managers can substitute players, but the captain decides on whether to kick for goal or to touch, or who takes the penalty. The manager works on a number of set plays, certainly, but he does not usually control when they are implemented.

When I was twelfth man for Kent during a close Sunday League game, I was told by the coach to carry out a message to the captain during the drinks break. 'Tell him from me that mid-off is too deep and to change the bowling from that end.' I dutifully relayed the message. The captain replied, 'Tell him to fuck off and let me captain the side. And tell him that's from me.' I passed on his words, or most of them. 'That's what I love about him,' the coach said immediately, smiling with genuine warmth. 'He makes his own mind up.'

But on other occasions, captains and players might welcome the extra help. Long before I played professionally, I remember watching Kent lose a big one-day match. Despite seemingly coasting to victory, we took a couple of inexplicable risks at the wrong times, holed out on the boundary, and put massive pressure on ourselves. We then lost both our nerve and the game. The Kent captain Chris Cowdrey later told me that if there had been a radio link-up from the coach to the players on the pitch, Kent probably wouldn't have lost. '"Just do nothing different and we'll win,"' he said, 'would have been the advice.' No wonder ex-South Africa coach Bob Woolmer tried to implement that system before the administrators stepped in to stop it.

It is a surprising comparison. America, which so values individuality and self-expression, has produced sports which are massively reliant on the intervention of coaches and managers, and a culture which demands players adhere to their demands. But in England, and in English-invented games worldwide, the players have hung on to more of their self-determination.

After the inter-squad game, I went to the locker room to meet the players. The first one I was introduced to, just as he was getting out of the shower, was Mike Piazza, the megastar of the Mets franchise. 'Ed, meet Mike,' was the intro, as though we were equals. 'Ed's a star cricketer from England, Mike.' When I explained about the book, Piazza sounded as though it was the best idea he had ever heard. 'What a great project, man! So tell me about this cricket stuff!' The Mets owner had just told me that Piazza easily recoups his $13 million a year salary by bringing huge PR value to the franchise. I was beginning to see why.

While the players tucked into an extensive range of post-match dinners – there didn't appear to be too much calorie counting going on – I wandered around the spacious locker room. You could almost fit Kent's whole 1st XI dressing room into the annex off the main Port St Lucie locker room where the coaches hang their clothes. And that's just a minor league ball park.

The Mets' weights room, adorned by the inevitable hip hop beats, reminded me more of Crunch, my $130 a month high-tech fitness centre in New York, than the cramped and old-fashioned gym at the county ground in Canterbury. And the weights the players were lifting? Suffice it to say that it would take about six cricketers pulling together to shift the mass of iron which one of the power hitters was repeatedly pumping.

The head coach's office, the data processing nerve centre of Operation Mets, was crammed with so many screens, video recorders and laptops that it could have been the security room of a blue chip office building. John Wright, who wanted to introduce a Statsmaster database while he was Kent's coach, would have killed for such a thorough means of study-ing his players.

To the side of the locker room was the kit area – a huge stockpile of virgin, still-in-the-packet T-shirts, trousers, belts, socks, shirts. I don't think the Mets players, as we do at Kent, get docked a cost-price fee every time they are given a replacement tracksuit. The Mets have several 'kit men', whose job it is to make sure the players' kit, and their locker room, look flawless every day. The one I met must do a very good job. After the Mets lost the 2000 World Series, they voted him a full share of the players' prize money pool, which worked out at over $300,000.

Sitting on a Mets-branded armchair among such luxuries, it was immediately clear that I had entered a whole new league of sporting franchise. The things we have to worry about at Kent – lost balls, missing kit – simply wouldn't register on the outflow statements at the Mets. When I took batting practice with the Mets, they wheeled out a skip-sized bin full of pristine Spalding baseballs. There must have been eight hundred balls in the bin – that's $30,000 of hand-stitched cowhide.

In England, sometimes getting hold of one practice ball that makes a half decent noise when you middle it can be difficult. At one stage last year the practice balls were so soft that one of the bowlers refused to bowl over 40 m.p.h. in the nets. 'Nothing personal, Eddie,' he explained as he lobbed a grenade-style delivery at me on the morning of a Championship match, 'but these things are blancmanges not cricket balls – I'm making a point.' The point was taken, and we got new warm-up balls for the next game.

Such problems are not unique to Kent. We are by no means a backward cricket club. But among English sporting organisations, only Premiership football clubs – perhaps only really Arsenal, Manchester United and Liverpool – are in the Mets' league. There is a lot of money in American sport, and a big slice of it is in baseball.

At one level I was jealous of the comfort, luxury and stage-hands. Cricketers often laugh about the privileges built in to other sports. When we play at Chester-le-Street in Durham, we share a car park with Newcastle United's state-of-the-art training ground. 'Do you think Alan Shearer will be jealous of my Renault Laguna?' I asked everyone. When we watch golf or soccer, a familiar joke is, 'Picked the wrong game, eh lads?' Not many of us really believe it though.

It is true that sportsmen want to practise and play in perfect conditions, leaving other people to concern themselves with the minutiae of logistical details. In theory, it means that the athletes can concentrate wholly on doing their job – batting, or pitching, or scoring goals, or whatever – with no tedious distractions. But I doubt that ever really happens. And how would sportsmen deflect their introspective thoughts without something to moan about? Whatever the conditions, we would probably eventually find new things to worry about.

Despite the signposts of success all around me, when I watched the Mets practise – really at work now – I saw how quickly the glamour fades when you are actually sweating away at the coalface trying to improve. No matter how many people watch you in big games, training and preparation is a relentless, unflashy business.

A morning rehearsal in the Royal Opera House scarcely resembles opening night; a rainy day on the Manchester United training field doesn't even hint at the experience of playing in front of a full house at the 'Theatre of Dreams'. No amount of money or facilities – though they certainly help – can bring intensity and atmosphere to training sessions. For the most part the players have to provide that themselves.

Looking around the Mets' locker room, I remembered Mike Brearley's suggestion that there are certain roles that need to be filled in any professional team. No matter what the group of people, they would end up positioning themselves in familiar roles within the culture of the dressing room. There would be a team joker, a team cynic, team loner and so on. Even when one of these types retires or leaves, someone seamlessly takes over his role.

Who were the equivalents in the Mets' locker room, I wondered, of Kent's great personalities?

It didn't take long to find my bearings. When I saw one locker full of muscle-building protein powders, energy pills, special training drinks and three pairs of running shoes, I thought I must have found the baseballing version of Paul Nixon, Kent's hyperactive fitness fanatic wicket-keeper. In the adjacent locker, I glimpsed a giant-sized Mars Bar. Ah ha! Mark Ealham's soul mate, I surmised.

Listening to Paul Nixon banter with Mark Ealham is one of my favourite dressing-room pastimes. One is full of wonder and amazement and infectious enthusiasm; the other is the epitome of commonsense, aware of the need to 'keep it simple'. Paul takes twenty food supplements every day to boost his energy levels (as if they needed boosting); Mark eats a bacon roll and says, 'In ten years' time, Nico, they'll prove all that stuff gives you cancer.'

If the Mets' Nixon and Ealham types revealed themselves easily, others might prove more difficult. No matter how hard

I searched, I doubted I would ever find the Mets' equivalent of Kent's mercurial left-arm spinner Min Patel – after all, I didn't know the name of the American version of the *Racing Post*, behind which Min is almost always concealed.

Others I was happy to avoid altogether. As a stranger, it might be dangerous to bump into the American Graham Cowdrey: he would almost certainly try to set your trousers on fire or tie your shoelaces together. The worst thing was that he'd always get away with it. When I played with Graham near the end of his career, he had managed to get himself in that enviable position where he could joke his way out of any situation. Even when he went too far – 'I don't care if it was Graham, you can't hide people's car keys and cut off their trouser legs' – you'd always end up laughing. It was amusing and exasperating in equal measure.

Did the Mets have a diarist type, I wondered, an intelligent but sceptical observer, someone like Somerset's Peter Roebuck, or the Yankees' Jim Bouton? I looked around unsuccessfully for a pile of serious looking books. People who enjoyed Roebuck's pithy county diary *It Never Rains*, incidentally, should read Bouton's *Ball Four*. Both are witty, honest and insightful. Bouton was the first baseballer to give the lie to the myth that baseball players were mostly well-behaved innocents. When he was summoned to see the Commissioner of Baseball, who demanded he issue a public apology admitting the book was full of lies, Bouton declined. *Ball Four* went on to sell 4,000,000 copies – the bestselling sports book of all time – and got Bouton banned from the Yankees' clubhouse.

Back in the locker room, when I saw a huge pile of baseball

bats, perhaps a dozen or more, I wondered if they belonged to the Mets' equivalent of Alan Wells. Perhaps this is a case of the pot calling the kettle black – I have a bat obsession too – but I never had as many as Alan. Even when I brought in last year's and lined them all up next to my new ones, he always seemed to have more – and that's just counting the ones he took out of his car. The worst part is that I always covet other people's bats, even though mine are usually brilliant, so I am always picking them up and wondering if they might make all the difference to my game. Having developed this comparative device, I could now go into any number of slanderous asides about my team-mates; easy targets, some of them. But how could I do that to my friends?

More to the point, who would be my equivalent, and by which characteristics would I recognise him? A very pleasant flight of fancy suddenly turned sour. What type am I? Sometimes I am in the thick of the piss-taking and the banter; other days, escaping with a book and my mobile, I play the recluse. Does that mean I am confused or just plain normal?

Fortunately such introspective thoughts were interrupted by Bobby Valentine, the Mets' manager. 'Good that you're here, Ed. I wondered when you were going to arrive. Let's get you in a uniform tomorrow morning and have you hit some baseballs. You'd better be good – we've heard all these fancy scouting reports from England and now we wanna see what you cricket*eers* are made of!'

No pressure then.

4

'A GODDAM CRICKETEER' HITS THE BASEBALL CAGE

This particular *cricketeer* had never before swung a baseball bat in anger. But when any cricketer picks up a baseball bat, even for the first time, in one sense he is returning to a more uninhibited, natural world, a world he has to some extent learned to forget. As a three-year-old, even a cricket-mad one, my cricket shots probably had more than a touch of the baseball swing about them. All those hours of cricketing indoctrination – 'straight bat', 'bat and pad together' – hadn't completely sunk in yet. And if you ask any normal, untutored person to take a swing at a ball, the result will almost certainly look more like baseball or golf than cricket.

Technique, in cricket as in anything, is partly about training an unnatural instinct to feel natural. But much as I hate to admit it to Americans, the raw full-blooded violence of the baseball swing is much closer to primal human nature than the refinement of the cover drive. Bigger, brasher, bolder – it's American. It is their Marlon Brando to our Cary Grant.

In many respects, I knew it was remarkably similar to being a batsman in cricket. The distance between the pitching mound and home plate, 60 feet, is almost exactly the same as the distance from one batting crease to the other. And the speeds of the major league pitchers are very similar to express fast bowlers. A 'heater' fast ball tends to be in the mid-90s m.p.h.; an express fast bowler tends to hover around or just below the 90 m.p.h. mark. Bowlers make up for the fact they have to keep their arm straight by being allowed a run-up, which pitchers aren't.

You don't have to be a genius to deduce from those facts that the reaction time for batter or batsman is very similar in both sports. A hitter has less than half a second – a 95 m.p.h. fast ball, for example, crosses the batting plate 0.4 seconds after it has been pitched. But crucial decisions, of course, need to be made much earlier. According to Robert Adair, professor of physics at Yale and a baseball theorist, batters have about 0.17 seconds to decide to swing. If they swing 0.0005 seconds too early, they will not have maximum bat velocity, and will be less likely to make good contact.

In *The Science of Hitting*, Ted Williams, perhaps the best pure hitter of all time, broke down that period of 0.4 seconds into three sections. 0.0 to 0.1: period of recognition; 0.1 to 0.25: period of decision to swing; 0.25 to 0.4: period of execution. I've never heard anyone talk about cricket reaction times in quite such scientific terms – we think of the *art* of batting compared to the *science* of hitting – but they would be almost identical.

The main difference is in baseball's emphasis on power. It is optional though useful for cricketers, but essential, at least in some measure, for baseball hitters. The baseball swing is an explosive uncoiling of a loaded spring. That's why seeing the power and violence of a full swing make clean contact with a high-speed fast ball is one of the most exhilarating things in sport.

The downside of baseball's emphasis on power is that it tends to produce less variety. Many of the best batsmen in cricket's history have been short, slight, neat. They deflected, evaded, timed, used the pace of the ball. That has not been the case in baseball. Not everyone is an out-and-out slugger, but the trend has always been towards bigger, stronger hitters. It's a home-run dominated game now. And you need to be seriously strong to hit home runs. The pitchers (who are generally still fairly normal looking specimens in terms of body shape) sometimes look like the kinds of guys that beefcake hitters might beat up in their spare time.

But no matter how big you are, you still need a certain amount of bravery at the batting plate. The first chapter of Leonard Koppett's *A Thinking Man's Guide to Baseball* begins with a one-word paragraph: 'Fear.' Pitching deliberately at the batter is illegal in baseball (unlike in cricket), but it does happen. The convention is that if a pitcher deliberately 'beans' a hitter, 'the dugouts empty'. The two teams don't necessarily fight; but they have to look as though they want to fight. All-for-one-and-one-for-all, and all that.

If the dressing rooms emptied every time a batsman got deliberately hit on the head in a cricket match there would be constant disruptions of play. A baseball batter might get hit if he's unlucky; a cricketer almost certainly will get hit if he hangs around long enough. It's a rare macho advantage I always enjoy pointing out to Americans: Yeah, they bowl at your head all the time. All part of the game. You just get on with it . . .

We are, admittedly, better protected. A baseball batting helmet has no cricket-style visor to protect your eyes, nose and mouth. It does cover your skull and leading ear; but if you duck into a 95 m.p.h. high 'inside' pitch – a beamer in cricketing parlance – there's nothing to get between your face and the hard, hide-covered ball.

When I bat in a cricket match, like all modern batsmen I nearly always wear a helmet with a metal grille that wraps around my face. Those of us who grew up wearing helmets – which only became commonplace in the late seventies and early eighties – can scarcely imagine what it must have been like without them. 'Getting in line' with only a cloth cap to protect your head meant putting your head in line with a potentially fatal hard, red ball.

It's difficult enough these days, when your life isn't at stake. Or shouldn't be. Even now, well protected by a helmet and grille, getting hit on the head is always a bit unnerving. In my second game of first class cricket, still full of myself after scoring a century on my debut, I was hit cleanly on the left ear by a bouncer from Dominic Cork – first ball. Back down to earth, quite literally, with a bang. I didn't think about it much at the time, but when I went to bed that night an intense earache kept me from sleeping on my preferred left side. How had I picked up earache only in one ear? Then I remembered being hit – my metal grille had prevented most of the damage, but had squashed my ear against my head.

Cricket batsmen also protect their bodies much more fully

than baseball batters. Like us, they do wear an abdominal 'box' protector, and a few baseball batters (though most don't) wear a protective pad on their front shin. By comparison, all cricket batsmen always wear full-length leg guards, padded gloves, and sometimes, on dodgy wickets or against fiercer bowlers, arm guards and chest pads. But we need it. It's a hard ball, son, and a hard game. And those straight-arm pitcher people are after us.

I'd thought for months about all these parallels and points of contrast, long before joining up with the Mets at Spring Training. So I wasn't a complete hick stumbling into a batting cage. I'd mugged up well at least. But if it's one thing understanding the business of baseball hitting, it's quite another thing doing it.

I felt strangely nervous when I turned up on my second day at Port St Lucie knowing I was about to have my first hitting workout. As a cricketer hoping to impress these baseball sceptics, I felt I was representing cricket in some broad and weirdly symbolic way. I might be the only cricketer they ever saw hit a ball. And if I was no good . . .

My transformation into a baseball player began with the serious business of getting kitted out. 'Don't just throw it on in any old order,' the kit man (he of the $300,000 bonus) told me. 'If you're gonna hit right, you gotta dress right.' I acquiesced: long black woollen socks first, then grey under-T-shirt, then shiny black Mets shirt, then spray-on-tight *Boogie Nights*-style polyester trousers complete with matching black leather belt. Now I understood why the baseballer Dick Stuart used to straighten his cap and tighten his belt before going out and then say, 'I add twenty points to my average if I know I look bitchin' out there.' With gear this tight, my Kent team-mate Dave Fulton would go straight to the nightclub from the clubhouse.

I couldn't stop smiling as I stood there, among the bats and discarded T-shirts of the Mets locker room – a cricketer turned baseballer. Why was I so happy? A couple of years ago, before I cared about baseball and before I had even heard of the Mets, wearing their kit would have meant nothing to me. I probably would have laughed at the idea. Silly game, stupid clothes.

But it's funny how following a team – admiring the way it plays, imagining yourself 'out there' – transforms simple garments like a shirt and a cap into something almost mystical. They become symbolic of a world that you can only enter via your imagination. Wearing the kit, which gives your imagination that extra nudge, is the closest you can get to realising the fantasy.

I hadn't experienced that childlike sense of wish-fulfilment for years. I felt the same as a boy when a Kent player gave me his county shirt at the end of one season. Dad told me I shouldn't wear it during school games because it would 'look like showing off'. But during the holidays I would put on the Kent shirt over my jumper and practise straight drives in the full-length mirror in my parents' bedroom. For those minutes, I *was* playing for Kent.

Now, ten years later and supposedly grown up, I was the Mets' clean-up hitter, off to 'explode into the ball', 'make some good cuts', 'get after those hanging pitches' and all those other things baseball hitters do. To spur me on, the Mets kit man was very nice about my new outfit. 'You look *great*,' he said, 'especially considering you're a cricket*eer*.' I never turn down a compliment, but I had become a little sceptical about Americans saying they liked what I was wearing. Dozens of shop assistants had said to me, 'Oh, it's sooo you, it's just a *must*' – even if I looked truly hideous. All part of the famous American charm, I began to suspect.

Dressed like a baseball player, I now had to learn to hit like one. That might be more difficult.

Before any game of cricket, I always walk out to the middle, take guard and face a few imaginary deliveries. The theory is that it makes you familiar with the pitch, the out-field, the sightscreens – so you acclimatise to match conditions. I did the same in the Port St Lucie baseball park. As I stood beside the batting plate, the first thing that struck me was how far away the fence was. It seemed miles away. How on earth did Mark McGwire hit seventy 90 m.p.h. pitches that far in one season? When you stand in the batter's box, the romance that has grown up around the home run becomes much more understandable.

In fact, it is 420 feet to the centrefield fence in Port St Lucie, which is, after all, only a minor league ground during the proper season. Some major league grounds are even larger. To hit a home run in even the smallest big league ground, you have to hit it further than you would to score a six at the Adelaide Oval – the longest straight boundary in cricket. No wonder baseball hitters work out – and strike out – so much.

The practice field at the back of the ground has similar proportions, but there is a batting 'cage' around the home plate area. That was where I was due to meet Mets manager Bobby Valentine to learn the basics of baseball batting.

I had tried several times to explain that I was 'just a county cricketer'. The message didn't seem to be getting across. Many Americans like to think they are dealing with someone special, so as my week in Florida progressed my cricketing achievements were inflated beyond all recognition. On day one I was 'an English cricket*eer*'; on day two I was 'an England cricket*eer*'; when I was introduced to the general manager of the LA Dodgers on my penultimate day in Florida, I was 'one of the best goddam cricket*eers* in the world'.

I promise I did nothing to propagate that myth. In fact, it made me feel distinctly uncomfortable, even fraudulent. But what can you do? Take people aside and say: 'Look here – you've got it all wrong, I play for one of the eighteen English counties, okay?' They weren't interested. They looked the other way. If the dynamic of a cricketer gaining privileged access to baseball was going to work, I had to play along with the image they wanted to pin on me – I had to play ball, I guess.

That settled, I allowed the whole 'star' thing to continue out of sensitivity to my hosts rather than any egotistical pleasure I might have gleaned from my new image. Somehow, though, I'm not sure my Kent team-mates would have interpreted it that way if they'd been listening at the time.

Another thing I noticed was how quickly the Mets slipped into bantering, dressing-room style familiarities with me. The first thing Bobby Valentine said to me as I walked through the locker room was, 'Look at the strut on this cricket*eer*! He's carrying a giant kit bag with cricket sticks and baseball bats and Mike Piazza's helmet. Geez, you've got a major league strut, boy!' Managers like Valentine, of course, who took the Mets to the play-offs in consecutive years for the first time in the history of their franchise, are celebrities every bit as much as their players. Because baseball managers are so involved in the game – making decisions, giving signals, calling plays – the TV cameras spend as much time focusing on them as on the players. They are not besuited backroom power-brokers. They are out there in baseball uniform working a sweat up.

A couple of batty looking Mets fans had waited all morning for Valentine to walk into the practice area. 'Could you sign our baseball please, Bobby?' He could. 'We're your biggest fans,' the couple added. 'But tell us – have you ever come across a player called Matt Williams? I think he used to be in the minors with the Mets.'

'The man who'll be able to help you with that is our new signing, who's standing right *here*,' Bobby said, pointing at me, encouraging a mischievous response.

'Oh, did you say Matty?' I asked confidently.

'That's right, Matty Williams, great third baseman . . .' While the man riffled through his Mets player profiles trying to work out who I was, his wife gasped excitedly at the prospect of hearing further news of Matty.

'No, sorry, doesn't ring any bells.'

That's one of the oldest games in sport. When someone is looking for something ('Has anyone seen my Calvin Klein watch?'), you say, 'A watch, a Calvin Klein one?' – as though you've got it in your hand. They get happy and excited and say 'Thanks, mate, I've been looking for that everywhere.'

Then you say 'no' dispassionately, provoking comic disappointment. Not my favourite pastime, I must admit, but it's a worldwide classic. And I walked off to the batting cage with a massively busy and successful manager who I had only known for five minutes, laughing at our practical joke. That's very typical of sportspeople.

Before I started hitting, I asked Bobby to explain the basics. 'The torque needed to hit a baseball 450 feet,' he began, 'comes from transferring your weight from your back leg to your front leg, snapping your front knee from bent to straight, and pivoting out your hips.' He played an air short, locking his front knee and twisting his hips emphatically. 'That gives more planes of movement, *moments* in the language of physics, than hitting with "arms only".'

Moments, physics, *torque*? I could only be in America.

'Show me your cricket swing,' Bobby asked, 'and we'll check out the different biomechanics.' I swopped bats and mimed a straight drive, which felt distinctly repressed and tame in comparison with Bobby's aggressive-looking baseball swing.

I explained that opening out my hips – what he was asking me to do with the baseball bat – is exactly what I try to avoid on the cricket pitch. It means I square up and either play across the ball to the on side or squirt it to gully. On the point of contact, of course, particularly on leg-side shots, your hips open out naturally. But if I square up as part of my preliminary movements, I'm in trouble.

'In baseball we need power, so pivoting your hips is essential,' Bobby explained. 'As a cricketer, you need to make consistent contact,' he added, displaying a beguiling understanding of cricket technique, 'so you should keep your hips and shoulders reasonably sideways and stable.' Just knowing the basics of a cricket batsman's task – to hit consistently and accurately – was enough for a baseball coach to deduce the elementary biomechanics.

Enough of the theory. Was I any good? First a few disclaimers. I didn't face Al Leiter pitching at 90 m.p.h. in my first trip to the batting cage. (Subsequently, I did face a few genuine fast balls, which were 'on me' before I had time to snap my wrists – meaning that I found it hard to hit properly to the leg side.) But this outing was more about learning the technique than experiencing the fear.

Having got that out the way, I can say that I did hit much better than I had anticipated. Perhaps I was inspired by the audience, which included the Mets' owner and assistant general manager, who were watching from behind the batting cage. Now that's an incentive: a few home runs here, I thought, and I could get signed up on one of those one-decade guaranteed $13 million-a-year mega contracts. So swing hard and enjoy!

'He's better than some of the guys you're paying in the minor leagues,' Bobby teased the Mets owner Nelson Doubleday. I didn't hit it nearly as far – surprise, surprise – as the 220-pound-plus power hitters like Mark McGwire and Mike Piazza. The balls I hit were only just about reaching the fence having bounced several times. The only time I got close to clearing it completely was when I sliced one 'out of bounds' – over backward point on a cricket field. It would be worth two runs in a cricket match; in baseball, it would count as a strike against me.

But I did make pretty good contact with most of the eighty

or so pitches. My spray chart showed that most of them landed in a straightish arc between what a cricketer would call wide mid-wicket and mid off. After only a few pitches, Bobby declared that I was a 'low-ball, inside hitter' – meaning I preferred them closer to my body and at about knee height. Just as well he didn't try to 'brush me back' with any high fast balls. I didn't fancy getting clocked with that cycling helmet on.

Even allowing for the considerable factor of American charm, I think the Mets management were a little surprised that an Englishman could get a baseball out of the batting cage, even if I couldn't – hard as I tried – clear the fence 420 feet away. 'Now that's what I call an athlete!' Bobby Valentine exclaimed at the end of my slugging session in which I had basically stood still and whacked it. I looked for signs of irony in his face, before remembering the different meaning of the word 'athlete' in America, where it means simply sporting aptitude rather than implying any actual *athleticism*.

And I would have settled for his conclusion that I was a 'low-ball, contact hitter'. Better to be a contact hitter rather than a no-contact hitter.

I should add that I am not the first professional cricketer to link up with a major league baseball team. My Spring Training trip was purely a reconnaissance mission; the Essex seam bowler Ian Pont went to the Philadelphia training camp in 1987 looking for a new job. His brother Keith, who set up the sponsorship deal which financed the trip, was quoted at the time as being amazed that the Phillies didn't sign up Ian as a pitching recruit.

'Ian was told he was better than half the pitchers on the

Phillies staff,' Keith explained. 'How can you tell someone that and then reject them? Speak to any of the coaches and the press and they'll tell you what a travesty this was.' An article in the *Tampa Tribune* put the other side of the story, asking, 'Who the hell does this guy think he is?' Travesty or not, that is as close as any modern professional cricketer has come to becoming a major league baseball player.

But that doesn't prevent us from imagining which cricketers might really excel on the baseball diamond. Even if it is too late for them to learn a new trade, which cricketers have the raw material to be great baseball players?

Among big hitters, Ian Botham would have been a natural. And I guess that Andrew Flintoff could cause some serious damage with a baseball bat. Inzamam-ul-Haq, too, one imagines, would not only make great contact, but also enjoy the low demands on aerobic fitness. There's no 'calling' either: if you hit it, you run.

Among fielders, I can imagine Paul Parker, the former Sussex captain who pioneered the one-motion slide-pick-up-and-throw in the early eighties, making countless baseball 'double plays' – effectively running out two batters in one ball. Chris Lewis, too, would have been a devastating baseball outfielder. Ricky Ponting, Herschelle Gibbs and Jonty Rhodes pick themselves as short stops, the baseball equivalent of cover point.

Catchers? The stereotypical catcher is burly, competitive and vocal. Wicket-keepers Ian Gould, Geoff Humpage and the late David Bairstow all had the perfect build and force of personality. As a pure hitting catcher, Adam Gilchrist would be difficult to beat. I add one non-wicket-keeper – Kent opener Robert Key, who is never short of a wisecrack and would have been a natural-born tobacco-chewer.

Pitchers are more difficult. Many cricketers have strong arms – Matt Maynard, Martin Bicknell, Simon Jones and Alex Tudor spring to mind among contemporary county players. But pitching demands a particular temperament. Perhaps Dean Headley, who could throw hard as well as bowl fast, and always liked to be considered a thinking bowler, would have enjoyed baseball's complex strategy.

But my top pick for a cricketer changing codes to baseball would be my Kent team-mate, Queensland and Australia's Andrew Symonds. His athletic fielding, huge sixes and up-and-at-'em approach would make him fit in, well, like a hand in a glove, in big league baseball. 'Why don't we just keep it simple, and watch the ball?' he tells us in the dressing room. Difficult to argue with that, Symmo, in either sport.

And which cricket legends are best saved for the cricket field? Most spin bowlers, of course, would find all those full tosses fairly unrewarding, though I'm sure Shane Warne's competitive drive would ensure he made his presence felt somehow. Bishan Bedi and Philippe Edmonds, on the other hand, might never overcome aesthetic objections to a game of hard throwing and frequent spitting. I am also happy not to imagine David Gower, Mark Waugh or Rahul Dravid at the batting plate. They would probably excel at anything to which they turn their attention, but somehow their languid style seems particularly suited to the cricket field and the cover drive.

It is, of course, a trivial game, trying to turn apples into oranges. But I allow myself one more imaginative jump: the

Don 'at the bat'. His pragmatism, efficiency and desire to eliminate weaknesses would have been ideally suited to the
science of hitting. Out of simple petty cricketing one-upman-
ship, I would love to have seen him whacking the best
pitchers of his day to all corners of a baseball field.

He made it as far as Yankee Stadium in 1932. Star attraction
Babe Ruth was meant to have played in the game, but an
injured leg enabled him instead to entertain the touring
Australians in his private box. So, in a rare connecting
moment in the histories of cricket and baseball, the two
greatest strikers of a moving ball got a chance to compare
notes.

The Babe and the Don. How apposite are their names. The
Babe – innocent, warm, unsophisticated, full of hope and yet
fatally vulnerable; the Don – shrewd, elevated, donnish. Born
at a similar time, they became the giants of their games,
whose lives of almost impossible brilliance coincided with
their respective nations' yearning for a hero and a superstar.

The Babe was a glutton, drunkard and hellraiser, but
beloved by almost everyone. He was born into poverty, edu-
cated at reform school, and constantly courted controversy
thereafter. The man known variously as the Bambino, the
Sultan of Swat, Wali of Wallop, Wazir of Wham, Maharajah of
Mash, Rajah of Rap, Caliph of Clout and Behemoth of Bust
died prematurely aged fifty-four. Beneath the excesses there
was melancholy and tragedy in Ruth's life, but not much mystery. He was an undisciplined but big-hearted ballplayer who
had been given an absurd talent. 'I hit big or I miss big,' Ruth
liked to say. 'I like to live as big as I can.'

Bradman, who was built more like a dancer than a bouncer,

remained as private and reclusive as the Babe had been extrovert and extravagant. He had few nicknames – no one ever really improved upon 'the Don'. If the Babe lived life like a schoolboy's dream, Bradman's achievements – in particular averaging nearly twice as much as the next best batsman – are somehow beyond even fantasy. How could he have done it? How could he have been so far beyond excellence? Those questions still reverberate wherever cricket is played. Even now, we are no closer to understanding how anyone in any sphere of achievement could have been so relentlessly brilliant. Just as Ruth suffered from a surfeit of humanity, Bradman's relentless consistency made him seem, through no fault of his own, somehow inhuman. When he died at ninety-two, the cricketing world was illogically surprised: we half imagined he might beat death too.

What a meeting it must have been in the Bronx in 1932 – the year that the Babe, in the twilight of his career, had performed his most fantastical feat, his 'called shot'. Heckled by Chicago Cubs fans during a World Series game at Wrigley Field, Chicago, he pointed to a corner of the crowd, then hit a home run over the centrefield fence to that exact spot. It must rank as sport's purest moment of childlike wish-fulfilment. Bradman was in his prime in 1932, and his fame was such that even the Babe, who could scarcely remember the names of his own team-mates, took a great interest in him. Bradman wrote in his autobiography that he found Ruth to be 'a typical American, but very curious about cricket'.

When the Don explained that you didn't *have* to run when you hit the ball in cricket, the Babe shouted, 'Just too easy.' 'Perhaps he was right,' Bradman reminisced about Ruth's boast, 'but I should have been delighted to see him try for a few minutes.'

But we never did get to see the Babe in batting pads, any more than Bradman 'at the bat'. Perhaps it is just as well. We would have been distraught had they turned out to be ordinary at anything, even an alien ballgame. But they did not escape comparison. When Bradman died in February 2001, the *New York Times* obituary, in a rare acknowledgement of cricket, worked out that over the course of a career a baseball batter would have to average .392 to be as far ahead of the pack as Bradman was from the next best Test batsman. Even the Babe couldn't manage an overall average of .392. Arguing about which is the greater game may be pointless; but cricket can be sure it had the greatest player.

Me? I had humbler ambitions in the baseball cage – primarily not humiliating myself in front of the Mets. I managed that much. Now I'm plotting to get my own back. What chance, I wonder, do I have of getting $13 million-a-year Mike Piazza to have a go in the nets at Canterbury?

5

'WAIT-WAIT-WAIT, QUICK-QUICK-QUICK'

A tennis-playing friend of mine insists that all ball sports share similar principles. Hitting a ball, he says, whether it be with a bat, club or racket, is a generic experience. Sometimes he asks me if I'm batting well. Whatever reasons I give for playing well or badly, he says: 'Hmm, exactly like my tennis – I told you about your head/hips/swing [delete as appropriate] years ago.' Often, though not always, he is right – certainly more often than I like to admit.

A golf pro, making a similar point, once told me that playing baseball is the best cure for a contorted golf swing. Hitting a baseball is fantastically liberating, he explained. 'You can't hit with clenched teeth' is a great baseball saying. It's true. You have to let go and trust yourself. Perhaps its remedial qualities extend to cricket, and I should go and hit a few baseballs when I'm having a bad trot – it might release some anger and get me back to swinging more freely. Okay, I admit maybe it wouldn't help the off-side shots too much.

But while I was at Spring Training I did half hope to pick

up some transferable advice about the general principles of batting. In case my coach is panicking reading this – 'Ed and his damned theories!' – I'm not planning to come back for the new season with a high baseball back lift or try to hit home run-style sixes over long on. But I was keen to find out how baseball hitters approached the three recurring themes of batsmanship: form, practice and technique.

Before I had ever even picked up a baseball bat, I remember being amazed at the relevance of a particular piece of batting advice. I was reading about the legendary contact hitter Tony Gwynn in George Will's book *Men at Work*. 'Wait-wait-wait', was his advice to baseball hitters, 'then quick-quick-quick'.

I read that piece of baseball advice in the middle of the 2000 season. Having had a fairly good year in 1999, and spent much of the winter thinking I was making improvements to my game, I started the new season disastrously. 0, 4, 24, 5: dropped; followed by 8, 0: permanently dropped. Rather than 'wait-wait-wait, quick-quick-quick', at the time my own batting was more like 'go-go-go, help-help-help'!

There's never a good time to be out of form, but it can be particularly depressing at the start of the season when there is no good sequence of scores to balance it out. Even when you find your touch again, you feel you are dragging it back, making amends, playing catch-up, trying to get back on an even keel. That's why most batsmen would give anything for some kind of decent score in one of their first few innings. Otherwise it can seem like an eternity before you get your season going.

Being dropped doesn't help either. So in 2000 I had to wait until August – *August!* some people already have a thousand runs by August – for my first real start, forty against Leicestershire. I thought I batted okay, but I was still playing too early, searching for the ball rather than waiting for it, maybe 'guessing' a bit then having to readjust, tiny errors sometimes, but they proved that I wasn't trusting myself.

So if I knew what was wrong, why couldn't I fix it? Hard as it is to believe, many struggling batsmen know what they're doing wrong. They even know what they should be doing right. But comprehension is only part of solving a problem; then you need to find the 'check', or cue, or phrase or metaphor that puts it right. That is why so many players go back to their fathers or their childhood coaches when they are out of form – to people who might not be the best qualified coaches in the world but who may have the knack of clicking their old pupil back into rhythm. Sometimes hearing someone else saying what you already know works wonders. That's why sportsmen sometimes attribute a successful day to seemingly random events or advice. Something happened that just helped them click.

I felt like that about 'wait-wait-wait, quick-quick-quick'. It probably only put more clearly and succinctly what I'd already been thinking about my game. But that's sometimes what good coaches and teachers do.

'Batters who have their hands out in front too early,' Gwynn explained, 'are finished by a pitch as soon as they are fooled by it.' In other words, if you can trust yourself for that extra second and play it a little bit later, you will give yourself a much better chance of getting 'out of jail', even when the bowler or pitcher has initially defeated you in the early stages of the ball's flight. That's the wait-wait-wait part.

Then, once you have properly located the ball, be quick-quick-quick. Make a clear decision – and quickly. Play or leave? (in both sports). Placement or power? (particularly in baseball). Forward or back? (in cricket). But that wait-wait-wait is so hard when you aren't in form because trusting yourself is the most difficult thing when you're short of confidence.

You get lots of advice from many different people, and sometimes it's difficult to be sure exactly what – if anything – helped you to turn the corner. Sometimes, it is a straightforward piece of luck, or just someone believing in you and transferring that faith.

So when I got 175 at Chester-le-Street in the next game, and waited for the ball a bit better, and moved a bit more quickly when I decided what to do, I couldn't be sure what had made the difference. Maybe Tony Gwynn and his 'wait-wait-wait, quick-quick-quick' had nothing to do with it. But I'm happy to give him some credit for providing that extra cue that helped me do what subconsciously I already knew I should be doing.

The whole issue of how you regain form is central to both cricket and baseball. Only a few sportsmen, the very lucky few, escape fluctuations in form. The rest of us have to hack our way through the bad times and learn how to 'put the wheels back on'. And the more quickly and efficiently you can identify the problem, if there is one, and rectify it, the more confidence you will have about 'fixing yourself' the next time you run into trouble.

Form is one of the great talking points in all games. When

do a couple of isolated failures turn into out-and-out 'poor form'? In baseball, at least, where batters are expected to fail on any given trip to the batter's box, the sequence is usually longer before 'poor form' is pronounced. In cricket, after just three low scores in a row you sense people are beginning to wonder if you have 'lost form'.

But have you? You might simply have nicked three good balls in a row. It could be no more complicated than that. We often forget how most innings, whether they turn out to be successful or not, begin in the same way: with some nerves and a few doubts.

Very occasionally, you do wake up in the morning and sense it is your day: the bat feels right in your gloves, the bowling seems unthreatening, the ball looks big. And it does turn out to be your day. Conversely, on other occasions, though you fight the emotion and try to conquer your negative thoughts, you feel it just isn't going to be your day. And it isn't. 'Never at the races today', you reproach yourself.

Much more often, though, a successful innings starts in exactly the same way as a failure. The difference? You don't get out, it gets easier, the tension subsides, you score runs. Otherwise, it is a carbon copy of the day on which you failed: the lead-up was the same, the outcome different. If you miss one ball in an innings you could argue you have been very lucky: if you had played it *better*, and nicked it, you would have been out.

The same could be said about an innings that ends in failure: it often starts in the same way as a success. The best I played in terms of technique, and the most secure I felt at the wicket in the whole of the 2001 season, was at Tunbridge

Wells. I really didn't miss a ball. Which was a shame, because the first one I didn't middle, I nicked. Out for twelve: an innings which felt as though it would be a big score. I lay on the dressing-room floor, reluctant to take off my pads, for about half an hour. I was trying to persuade myself not to think about the nick any more than I would have thought about it had I missed it – and survived to bat on. It is the shot, after all, not the outcome, that warrants analysis. That is the rational view. But who can be rational when he is out?

It was the kind of day that reminds me about how crazy cricket can be. Perhaps that is why so many players have that phlegmatic look about them. As Daryll Cullinan said to me on another day after I got a frustrating forty-odd: 'You've got to be philosophical as a batter. Otherwise it's torture.'

Was I just unlucky today? Have I lost form? Do I need to change something? If so, how? Getting the answers right to those questions, whatever your sport, is harder than it sounds.

When you've *really* lost form it is difficult even to *imagine* scoring runs. It's like being in a snowstorm and trying to remember what a summer's day feels like. Your rational side knows that summer days aren't that difficult to imagine – you've lived through plenty of them, after all. Your irrational side feels only the cold.

If you're not careful, it's even possible to catch yourself watching players who you would normally consider ordinary and saying to yourself: how does he do it? How does he get to *seventy*? I used to play with a sublimely gifted batsman who used to find losing form almost unbearable. One day while we were watching our numbers ten and eleven put on a small stand, he looked particularly mortified. When our number ten hit a nice but unremarkable straight drive, he pulled my arm as if he was about to fall over, looked despairingly at me, and blurted out, 'I used to be able to play that shot, I really did.' He still could, of course, better than any of us, but he had forgotten his gifts – and all he could see was other people's facility and his failure.

Different people have different theories about getting back into form, sometimes extraordinary ones. When I played against Australia in 1997, our first three batsmen – me included – got nought. So in the second innings we were all on 'pairs'. One of the other guys on a pair pulled me aside before the start of play to ask me, 'So how are we going to approach these pairs? Are we going to slog one early and get off 'em that way, or block it until we get a bad ball?' He was joking, I think, but not entirely.

One of the problems with losing form is that you try too hard, and often in the wrong ways. You bat with too much desperation. You lower your backlift, grip the bat tighter, use a shorter swing, don't follow through with your hands, 'come off' shots early. But the siege mentality – 'I'm not getting out, I'm not giving it away, I am not taking any risks, I *will* get my form back' – often merely serves to make you hit the ball even worse. 'Batting as though their life depends on it', as most batsmen have been advised to do at some point, sometimes just makes them even jumpier.

The whole issue of form influences the way we practise. The temptation there, too, is to eliminate risk. I'm out of nick, you say to yourself, so I can't get out in a net. Be tight, compact, risk-free – none of which are bad in themselves. But bit by bit, you can lose contact with the rest of your game. So when you're playing a match and someone serves up a juicy half-volley, instead of hitting it to the boundary as you have been doing since you were ten, you blouse it to mid off. Then it's easy to get down on yourself. And if you're not careful you can slip back into the self-defeating cycle of playing against yourself as well as against your opponent.

So some people – and I'm certainly no expert here – say that a way of regaining touch, and getting around all those problems, is going back to playing more naturally in certain forms of practice. It doesn't even need to be organised practice, where you will be analysed and assessed all the time. It could be anywhere. I know one coach, a sort of batting doctor, who has a reputation for being able to 'fix' struggling batters. He gets you to hit balls rolling slowly along the ground with a golfing-style 'free, uninhibited swing'. He repeats the phrase over and over again: 'free, uninhibited swing'. Be natural, be fluid, be like you were as a child. He even gets batsmen to hit front-footed square cuts off full-length balls outside off stump – one of the most demanding shots in cricket. It is the shot you are least likely to play in a game when you are out of form. 'But playing it,' he says, 'demands that you get yourself in a good position to hit the ball properly. It doesn't matter that you won't play it in a game.' You are practising a skill-demanding shot to get the essentials right for easier ones.

In the middle of one mediocre run of scores, I was frequently out caught behind the wicket. Lots of people thought I should cut out off drives. I went along with received opinion, didn't practise it and kept on nicking out. Then I decided

I would go back to practising it rather than cutting it out of my game. I got my dad to chuck me a few forty-mile-an-hour balls in the back garden. With no one looking, I hit them properly for the first time in months. I got runs from then on to the end of the season.

In search of their 'feel', getting their timing and bio-mechanics just right, baseball players often do hours of seemingly entirely unrealistic batting practice. In terms of grooving their swing, they hit balls more like I do with my dad than I do in competitive net practice. In fact, one of my biggest surprises at Spring Training was how little hitters practise against top pitchers at full tilt. That's called 'live' batting practice, and it doesn't happen very often. Why?

First, the number of pitches thrown by every pitcher is carefully monitored. On the wall in the coaches' changing room – they have their own area, set slightly apart from the mass of players – there is a list of the number of minutes each pitcher has thrown on every day of Spring Training. 'Al Leiter – Monday 17th: 10mins, Wednesday 19th: 6mins, Friday 21st: 8mins.' Even the minor leaguers and trialists have a column full of precise entries. Most of that work is done one on one with a catcher or pitching coach, concentrating on hitting the right areas of the strike zone and getting good movement ('action') on the various pitches. Batters swinging at the pitches might just confuse the issue. As one of the pitchers told me, 'My primary aim is to throw my fast ball with plenty of heat into the right area – after that it's in the lap of the gods.'

Secondly, the batters aren't always very keen to practise against 'good stuff' in 'live' batting practice. They might do some early in Spring Training to get back into the feel of swinging against seriously fast pitches, or after making a recovery from injury. But for most of the time many batters are content to practise against 'dead arm' pitching – slow, unrealistic pitches thrown by batting coaches. They want to groove their swings, not get knocked about, so their practice is focused on developing correct muscle memory for clean hitting. As a result, you see these phenomenally powerful athletes swinging themselves off their feet at very friendly-looking pitches – while the batting coach, having lobbed up another pitch, runs for cover behind a mesh fence.

Most cricketers oscillate during the season between practising in match-style nets or middle practices and much easier half-volley 'throw downs'. Some batsmen say: give me the most realistic practice I can get, and as often as possible. 'Practise as we play' is their motto. They like nets on the morning of matches to be as realistic as possible; they like to smell the leather as it passes under their noses.

Others prefer to whack half-volleys thrown from 10 yards away by obliging fellow batsmen. They try to take that feeling of hitting every one with the meat of the bat out into the middle, even though they know conditions will be very different. Sometimes, just hitting one absolutely right is all they are aiming for.

Most batsmen probably mix up the two, doing enough throw downs and batting drills to feel they are hitting the ball well, but not neglecting realistic practice. Most of the time, batsmen are only too keen to put their hands up for a net. It's the bowlers, who have all the hard work to do, who look less convinced.

And me? I like to bat, I suppose, against whoever will bowl

or throw. I've always been unable to resist the offer of a bat, even when I don't need one. As a boy, I would say to my father after an hour in the nets, 'Just ten more, Dad.' But batting was a toy I never wanted to part with. So after the tenth, I always made sure four balls were resting near his feet: 'Just those near where you're standing, then.' I could never have enough of that sort of practice.

Most batsmen are probably working at two levels when they practise. In the immediate term, they are trying to prepare for the next game. They are seeking ways to maintain or regain that all-important commodity 'form'. But at a broader level, they will probably also be working on longer-term improvements in their technique. They will be trying to use their feet more against spin, or play more fluidly on the back foot, or transfer their weight better into their drives.

The irony is that when you are 'in form' your technique tends to work pretty well. And when you're out of form, your technical shortcomings become apparent. But sometimes working too hard on technique when you're short of form and in the middle of the season can make you still more preoccupied and confused. You can end up thinking about your feet or your pick up instead of watching the ball. So when is the best time to work on purely technical issues? When you're in form, right, and full of confidence? But then aren't you guilty of tampering with something that is working fine, and guilty of breaking the old 'if it ain't broke, don't fix it' adage?

And then you have to weigh up how much technique you really *need*, however you might go about achieving it. After all, some of the best players in cricket and baseball, like Ty Cobb, have had distinctly imperfect techniques. They worked out their own game, and which parts would never be perfect, and stuck to it. 'Don't get fucked up on technique, Ed, for Christ's sake,' one coach used to say to me. 'It's having it in *here* [pointing at his head] and in *here* [pointing at his heart] that counts.' Almost certainly true, but where does that leave your back defence?

It's when I'm in the middle of trying to work through decisions and judgements like all those that I sometimes think to myself: I wish I was one of those purely instinctive sportsmen who never give any of these things a second thought. But there's no point trying to be someone you aren't. You've got to be yourself, I guess – only better!

For all its pitfalls, learning about technique is part of my fascination with sport. But given that we can all usually agree on what good technique looks like when we see it (as exemplified by Greg Chappell, Martin Crowe or Sachin Tendulkar), there is surprisingly little unanimity about how to get there. That's why sportsmen frequently argue about technique, about why this works, or that doesn't.

Some people have such strong views about technique that two players may watch the same shot and see two entirely different things. The shot might even be your own. I once watched a video of myself batting in a net practice with someone who had a technical suggestion for me. The actual question was: was my head falling over to the off side? The underlying question was: does it matter if it does a little bit? He slowed the video down, frame by frame, until I was moving the bat about a millimetre each second. We stared eagerly at my head. 'See, see! It's going, it's going!' he said. 'Now . . . wait for it . . . now . . . err . . . you see!' I didn't. It looked still – still enough, anyway. My adviser was tearing his hair out.

Admittedly, it is rare to disagree on what actually happened. It's much more common to disagree on *why* it happened. One pre-season in South Africa, we were having a team barbecue when the India vs Australia highlights came on television. The whole squad of twenty players rushed into the captain's room to watch. Tendulkar made forty off about twenty-five balls and played with superhuman brilliance. After a couple of Castle lagers, we oohed and aahed at the extravagant drives 'on the up'. 'See, it's simple. It's all about his head and his hands,' Alan Wells said, pointing at his head then his hands to underline the point. 'The main thing is he's not squaring up at all,' another added. 'Above all, his balance is perfect,' someone else chipped in.

We were drunk and happy enough to think we were all agreeing. The three contributors even nodded enthusiastically at the others' technical explanations. And, of course, they were all right to some extent. He was doing everything perfectly, so you could take your pick from a whole lot of technical qualities. It was the emphasis that differed. We were all seeing the same shot through different eyes, and we were explaining it with different emphases on different points. In fact, we were trying to believe the key to Tendulkar's batting was the same as the key to our batting. He might be better than me, people were thinking, but I'm not barking up the wrong tree – am I?

Differences in opinion also express themselves in the way people talk about 'keeping it simple'. Everyone claims to keep it simple. It's the first thing any coach says: 'Now I want to keep this really simple, because it's a simple game made complicated by us lot . . .' What does keeping it simple mean? Usually, it means stressing one or two points above all others. People who emphasise two different points are 'making the whole thing too complex'. The fact is sometimes very simple advice will work: Tony Gwynn's 'wait-wait-wait, quick-quick-quick' was pretty simple. But the entire art of batsmanship, no matter what anyone tells you, cannot be summed up in two or three, or thirty words. It's too difficult. The end product might appear simple; it might even come naturally to some; but the skills themselves aren't always that simple – and fitting them all together into a whole game certainly isn't. If it was that simple, we'd all be doing it right.

That's not to say we should make things complex for ourselves. There comes a point where you have to draw the line and say, 'I've done enough watching and learning and thinking for the time being – I'm just going to play now.' It's amazing what self-confidence can do – and some people want to protect theirs from too much round-the-table discussion. 'What's the cure for a batting slump?' runs one baseball saying. 'Two pieces of cotton wool – one for each ear.'

I was never going to follow that advice all the time. And I've listened to dozens of technical theories, trying to sort out the ones that might help me from the plain wrong. In a way, I'm glad I plunged myself into it. At least now I know a bit more about when to listen and when to reach for the cotton wool. Because somewhere along the line you have to sort it out for yourself. It's all about (delete as appropriate) your head/hands/hips/heart . . .

6

BAT VERSUS BALL

A ny game which encompasses a variety of different disciplines will be prone to arguments about which ones are
the hardest to perform. A common debate among cricketers is
whether the game is easier for batsmen or bowlers. Batting,
the bowlers say, is a picnic. You stroll out to the middle, enjoy
smacking the ball around while expending little energy and
experiencing almost no pain, then come back to the pavilion
and put your feet up. If it's not your day, there's even more
time to rest up. Poor bowlers, on the other hand, particularly
fast bowlers, have to toil away in all weathers, up hills, into
gales, and through injury.

Just as rugby union forwards are always telling their airy-
fairy three-quarters about where the real battle is done,
bowlers like to lecture batsmen about the pain barrier, keeping on going, and how there's nowhere to hide. They suspect
the whole game is organised for the benefit of precious,
posing batsmen. As one of England's greatest seam bowlers,

Sir Alec Bedser, used to say, 'When was the last time a bowler got knighted?'

Batsmen don't tend to see the game in those terms. Their trump card is the 'one-chance' argument. Yes, they say, bowling is hard work. And we really do appreciate all the hard slog you guys put in for the team. Didn't you hear me encourage you from the soft grassy area at mid-off as you recovered from slamming your delivery leg into the concrete-hard wicket? In Clintonian or Blairite rhetoric, 'We feel your pain.'

And what about us? We only get one chance at the wicket. We could get an unplayable ball first up, or a wrong decision, or just a piece of bad luck. And can we turn back to our mark and run in again? Can we put it all behind us and focus on the next ball? No chance: it's 'goodnight Charlie', as the commentator Tony Greig likes to say. Is it any wonder we are a bit prone to melancholic introspection and occasional temper tantrums? You should try it . . . no, not just any old batting, we know you do that as well as bowling, but *primarily* batting – it does funny things to your mind.

Bowlers counter by saying that the whole evolution of the game has favoured batsmen. Covered wickets, originally meant to ensure more play for the paying spectator, made batting easier by flattening out the surface (though many contemporary English county batsmen would point out that there seem to be plenty of seaming tracks around at the moment).

The front-foot no-ball rule, meanwhile, stopped bowlers from 'stealing' that potentially crucial extra yard or two of pace by 'dragging' their back foot. And now there's that 'red zone' on Channel 4, bowlers say, you never get a bloody LBW decision – it looks worse for the umpire if he 'gives him' and he's not out, than if he 'gives the benefit' and it looks 'close'. Everything's moved in favour of the batsman . . .

I'm not so sure. We gave bowlers a third stump in 1775, didn't we? Before then, if the ball passed between the two stumps without dislodging the bail, it was deemed 'not out'.

A similar argument has always existed between baseball pitchers and batters. Pitchers, it is often said, are prone to paranoia – suspecting, like bowlers, that the game is skewed in favour of spoilt, glory-boy batters, who do none of the hard slog and get all the credit. It is certainly true that whenever the ball has had a period of dominance in baseball history, the law-makers have stepped in to help the batters in distress.

The 1968 season, for example, saw the pitchers' greatest moment – but also the beginning of their worst nightmare. The major league batting average was .237, the lowest ever, and the average number of runs per game fell to 6.84. The following year, they lowered the pitcher's mound from 15 inches to 10 inches, and shrunk the strike zone. Five teams also moved their fences in.

The result? In 1969, there were three times as many .300 hitters as there had been the year before, and the number of hitters who struck forty or more home runs rose from one to seven. It was not the first time the law-makers have intervened to make baseball more hitter-friendly, nor will it be the last.

Baseball knows on which side its bread is buttered – the side of batting, or, as it is known in baseball, 'offence'. That is the people's choice. The typical fan likes to see big hitting home runs in the baseball park, not scoreless 'shutouts'. No wonder the pitchers feel a little threatened. As legendary Dodgers pitcher Orel Hershiser put it, 'There never has been a rule change that helped the pitcher.' Most pitchers would see more than a grain of truth in the satirical magazine article which attacked their whole breed: 'If we eliminated pitchers they wouldn't be missed: they are pampered little swine with no real effect on the game except dragging it out and interrupting the action.'

The batters, needless to say, see things differently. Hitters think that making contact with a small ball hurled at over 90 m.p.h. from only 60 feet away is the hardest task in sport. As veteran manager Jim Frey used to say, 'the average big league hitter is a struggling hitter. If you're at .250 or .260, where most players find themselves, it never comes easy. You have to go out and grind it out, day after day, just to stay at that level. A .250 hitter hits one ball good every night, and if it happens to go right at somebody, he's in trouble.'

Even the very best of us, say baseball batters, average only around .300. Which other group in society has to endure failing seven times out of ten in the full glare of public scrutiny?

During Spring Training, I chatted to Todd Zeile and Robin Ventura – two of the Mets' starting hitters – and told them about the playful antipathy between batsmen and bowlers in cricket. 'What do baseball batters think of pitchers?' I asked. 'Well, the first thing you have to understand about pitchers is that they're non-athletes,' Zeile joked. 'All they can do is throw. That's the whole athletic package. Throwing, throwing and *throwing*.'

'They think they can hit, too,' Ventura added. 'They can't. In fact, I suspect they only took up pitching as kids because they never hit the damned thing!' It all sounded very like my rugby-playing fly half room-mate. 'I love forwards,' he would say after the game, looking distinctly spritely and unmarked by the scars of conflict, 'so long as they give me the ball and don't get any delusions of grandeur. They're only there, after all, because they couldn't run as children so they were told to push instead.'

Even the cockiest fly half or batsman doesn't really believe that – well, not completely – but the banter between the practitioners of a game's different disciplines is one of the funniest parts of playing sport. I used to play with a really dogmatic 'it's-a-bowler's-game' batsman. When I was out and needed cheering up, I would occasionally try to induce him to explain *why* it's a bowler's game. 'No question, absolutely no question,' he would say. 'We only get one chance, one chance, *one bloody chance* . . .' Sometimes, I'd already finished my coffee and packed up my kit by the time he'd finished chanting 'one chance, one chance' to himself. In truth, I know the feeling.

Batsmen also have to put up with listening to bowlers in the dressing room before and after they bat. You quickly discover that bowlers don't care who gets the runs. Nor are they interested in whether they're made well, or luckily, or stylishly. They just want the batsmen to do their job.

When I played my first games for a new team, one of the bowlers approached me after net practice. 'I'm so glad you're playing,' he began – how kind, I thought – 'because one of you batters has got to get some bloody runs, and the rest of them aren't going so well.' A logic, I reflected, that might not always be used in my favour.

Worst of all, never let a bowler hear you talk about form, unless you're actually in it. 'I feel in great form, honestly, I mean I'm hitting the ball so well in the nets . . . it's just the runs in the middle that aren't coming.' This tends to provoke their most aggressive responses – 'I don't care how you get them so long as I can see them on the scoreboard, which currently I *can't* . . .'

Runs mean time at the wicket for the batting side, which for bowlers means time spent not bowling, which facilitates hot baths, the physiotherapy bench, and rest – all preferred pastimes among bowlers.

Sometimes bowlers get extra anti-batsman encouragement from disenchanted coaches. Once I played in a team where the coach was a former batsman, who, try as he might, didn't seem able to get the batsmen to make more runs. The more he helped, the less runs they made. This disappointed him. Not only that, they kept getting out the same way. This enraged him. Worse still, some of the batsmen still talked about 'hitting the ball well'. This was going too far.

Eventually he started spending more of his time with the bowlers. They did what you told them. If you said 'bowl outside off stump', they did. If you said 'the batsmen are useless', they agreed. Those batsmen, on the other hand, full of damned theories . . .

Bowling – a proactive enterprise – is a more exact science than batting. Bowlers can only try to bowl the ball in the right place (something they can even practise doing on their own); what happens after they've let go of the thing is out of their control. As someone who has tried bowling, and, to put it generously, has been found wanting, I am not saying bowling is easy. Nor would I change places with them for any money. I'm just saying bowling is more scientific and more controllable.

Batting, on the other hand, is not such an exact science. You are responding to something which you cannot control: a ball, delivered from a slightly different angle than last time, at a slightly different place, moving in a slightly different way.

You cannot be thinking about where you will hit the ball before it is bowled – because if you do it has a terrible habit of being in the wrong place. This makes batting, and batsmen, difficult to bank on. The truest cliché in cricket is that any batsman can get out to any ball.

No wonder coaching batsmen is a difficult business. You can't *tell* them to do or think anything – because when the ball arrives they can't be thinking anything apart from watching the ball. You have to make them see things for themselves, in their own way; to change subtly their subconscious mindset; to reprogramme the hard drive. (Am I scaring off any potential batting coaches here?)

It's the same in baseball. When I spoke to the Mets coaches in their changing room before a game against the Los Angeles Dodgers, I asked one of them, Mookie Wilson, if he was the batting coach. 'You must be kidding,' he laughed. 'That's much too difficult for me. I'm much happier as first base coach. Batting coach – imagine . . . God no!'

I was also interested to hear Mookie Wilson say that most batting slumps are caused by mental rather than physical problems. 'Nine times out of ten, batters lose form because they lose confidence not because their swing has gone. It's fixing their confidence that's so difficult.' Even if it's not working, he was saying, it might not be broken.

If batters in both games face the prospect of periodic slumps – and the accompanying avalanche of advice and fits of introspection – at least not many of them suddenly completely 'lose it'. Over time, their performances taper off, maybe – but rarely do they evaporate immediately.

But the flipside of bowling (and pitching) being proactive rather than reactive is that it is susceptible to 'the yips'. The yips are a golfing phenomenon; the term referring to the inability to complete your putting action smoothly. The time you spend hovering over the putt becomes too much to bear, and you fluff it – over and over again. It is a psychological disaster that can happen to anyone. The problem lies in dwelling on the prospect of failure. So the yips only strike when you have enough time to think. Time can be a sportsman's worst enemy.

Spin bowlers have traditionally suffered from the yips. Even Middlesex and England's Phil Edmonds, with his perfect left-arm orthodox action, had a bout. At a somewhat lower level, I too got the yips. Not in professional cricket, thank God, when they only throw me the ball to have a laugh when the game is dead – but as a schoolboy when I fancied myself as an all-rounder.

Pitchers, too, get the yips. I watched a rookie pitcher suffer hideously from the yips on the biggest night of his career, pitching in the 2000 play-offs. He was throwing it over the batter, past the catcher, into the crowd. It was terrible just watching it. No one knows yet whether it will come back when he is next under that kind of pressure. That is one affliction, at least, that rarely happens to cricket batsmen or baseball hitters.

The argument between bat and ball in cricket extends to the nature of the surface on which the ball bounces – one aspect of baseball which doesn't change that much, because the ball doesn't bounce. Of all the bowler's complaints, a really flat wicket, particularly on a hot day, brings out their most trenchant views. 'If that thing was any flatter,' they say, 'there'd be catseyes and white lines running down the middle of it.'

In fact, it is ironic that both batsmen and bowlers often devote considerable energy to arguing about how the wicket is perfectly suited to the other discipline. 'What a great day to be a bowler' batsmen say as they lay eyes on a green wicket. Some post-match chats hinge on the state of the wicket. 'But was it really seaming that much?' the bowlers ask. 'It seemed pretty flat when we were bowling on it.'

If it really *is* flat, there will be no end to the complaints. Horizontal on his dressing-room bench at tea, with 0 for 85 under his belt, and a 'sidecar' (the wrong kind of hundred) looming, a bedraggled bowler will occasionally turn to the fresh-looking batsmen, as yet largely unhurt by the day's exertions: 'If you lot can't score a hundred each on that bloody motorway of a wicket, with no cloud cover to help the ball swing, and not a blade of grass for movement off the seam—'

It is not a good time for a batsman to drop a catch.

So batsmen and hitters and bowlers and pitchers do share many characteristics – not least a playful antipathy towards the practitioners of the other discipline.

But, and I hope this is not one parallel too many, in many respects the real equivalent of the baseball pitcher is the cricket batsman, and the real equivalent of the baseball batter is the cricket bowler.

At the most fundamental level, baseball is a pitcher's game and cricket is a batsman's game. The cricket batsman is expected to win any one particular ball: no matter how bad the batsman or how good the bowler, it is nearly always more of a surprise when a ball produces a wicket than when it does not. Dots and runs are the bread and butter of cricket; wickets are the exceptions.

In baseball hits are the exceptions and strikes the norm. The pitcher wins most pitches and the hitter hopes to hang in there long enough to capitalise on a mistake.

That role reversal does strange things to the dynamics of pressure in baseball and cricket. Though there is great pressure (which can often lead to psychological torment like the yips) on bowlers, most cricketers accept that the pressure on batsmen is even more concentrated. The one-chance issue comes up here again. But so too, ironically, does the extent to which the odds are stacked in the batsman's favour. Getting out becomes more terrible in prospect the less it is acceptable. That explains the paradox of why there is less pressure on batsmen when you play on terrible pitches. Wickets are devalued, so losing one is not such a disaster. That is not to say batsmen like playing on bad wickets, as they will all tell you at great length.

But whatever the wicket, few sporting experiences compare in terms of pure pressure with starting an innings. The finality of dismissal, which looms so large at the start of a batsman's innings, is one of cricket's most macabre fascinations.

By now you will have guessed where I am going with this. The equivalent pressure in baseball is on the pitcher. The rarity of a pitcher giving up a run in baseball makes it more catastrophic even than losing a wicket. Meltdown in cricket is the batting collapse; meltdown in baseball is conceding a series of home runs.

Why? Because pitching errors (i.e. giving up runs) exert their dramatic impact on the game so much more quickly than hitting errors. In baseball you cannot *not* score runs in a hurry. Being 'hitless' is a process, an unhappy one certainly, but a process all the same. You don't click your fingers and find yourself on nought after nine innings. Likewise, it often takes hours, sometimes days, to lose control of a cricket game when you are in the field. Very occasionally, a few big hits might change the whole course of the match. Much more often, it slips away from you in ones and twos and the odd four. 'They're getting going here' becomes 'we could do with a wicket' becomes 'we need a wicket' becomes 'they are on top' becomes 'we are out if it'. A slow death by asphyxiation.

By the same logic, it is obvious that the cricket batting team can lose the match in a few balls, and the baseball pitcher in a few blows. Ironically, in many respects the state of being the pitching team in baseball or the batting team in cricket gives you control of the game. Moderate success is the status quo. But failure, when it comes, is much worse. It is always more sudden and often more final. It is death by guillotine.

The comparison between cricket batsmen and baseball

pitchers extends to the manner of their exit. The decapitated body has to be removed ignominiously from the field of battle. If a pitcher is giving up too many runs, his manager will make a 'call to the bullpen', which means calling upon one of his relief pitchers from the subs bench to finish the job that his starter couldn't manage.

Sometimes, a pitcher will be replaced even if he has pitched well. It is no more than replacing a tired throwing arm with a fresh one. But other times, the replaced pitcher feels chronically snubbed. He cannot be trusted to do the job required. The manager will often walk out to the mound to console him. He often looks inconsolable. It all reminds me of the cricket batsman's slow 'what-have-I-done?' walk back to the pavilion.

When I started to get interested in the pitcher, not just the hitter, I began to enjoy baseball at a completely different level. If you wait for the hitter to hit, it can be a long night. But if you follow the pitcher, and sense how the guillotine blade is inching towards his neck with every ball, walk and base hit, baseball offers a cumulative build-up of pressure that few sports can match.

A score of 0-0 after nine innings sounds a boring game. And it might be – if the pitcher had thrown strikeout after strikeout, rather like a tennis star serving skilful but unplayable aces at will. But it might have been utterly absorbing if the pitcher had faced the potential game-losing threat of the bases being loaded in every innings. Pitching is like serving to stay in the match, every game, every day. Yes, the odds are in your favour. But the pressure is on your back.

So, as a cricket batsman, my sympathies are divided at baseball games. In terms of skills, I feel much closer to the hitter. In terms of mental state, I feel much more affinity with the pitcher. It's a dual allegiance I very much enjoy.

7

UNDERSTATE, OVERACHIEVE

I certainly had comfortable surroundings in which to consider my dual allegiance to pitchers and hitters. In fact, lying poolside in Jupiter Island recovering from my first workout as a baseball hitter and hearing reports of torrential rain and sleet in east Kent, the prospect of a prompt return seemed like the second best option available. Worse still, the Mets owner mischievously offered to fax Kent to say that I had suffered a rare and debilitating injury which allowed me to swim, play golf and swing a baseball bat but not play cricket. One more Southsider cocktail and I might have agreed. I had to get out of Florida quickly . . .

I did successfully manage to wave goodbye to the Mets and the good life and drag myself to West Palm Beach airport just in time to get back for pre-season. The county ground was now so wet that Kent had abandoned hope of playing any cricket at Canterbury for weeks. In one of the happiest team meetings I have ever attended, club captain Matthew Fleming announced that we were flying away for a pre-season training camp. The choice was between Antigua, Port Elizabeth and Bombay, where, ironically, I had already spent several productive weeks playing cricket earlier that winter. South Africa won, and within three days I was on my fifth long-haul flight in two months.

In 'pro' parlance, Port Elizabeth was 'hard yakka'. We knew it wouldn't be a holiday when Matthew Fleming advised us not to bring too many casual clothes – assuring us that we would be squeezing every possible drop of cricket practice into the ten-day trip. But the joy of batting on decent wickets (in March, too) and the comparative comfort of doing catching practice in above-zero temperatures meant no one minded working hard.

On most evenings, after practice, all I was good for was a trip to the internet café and a surf around the Mets' website. That would be a feature of my entire summer: checking up on the Mets every day, monitoring the graph of their season compared to ours. I liked doing it. It was a new way of getting through rainy days in the dressing room, a new focus to take me away from dwelling on last-over defeats.

How had their Spring Training finished up, I wondered, after I had left? Extremely smoothly, seemed to be the answer. When they won a warm-up game, it was a good omen. When they lost one, their web reporter suggested it was good to get such defeats out of the way when it didn't matter. Pitchers were talking up batters, batters were talking up pitchers, coaches were talking up everyone. ('If there was an award for the best pitcher in the whole of baseball this Spring Training,' Bobby Valentine announced, 'Al Leiter would win it.') Team spirit was excellent, no stone was being left unturned. It's amazing: take away competitive matches in which you have a 50 per cent chance of losing, and almost every sporting team does swimmingly. It must be something about the spring.

It is scarcely surprising that a team which had lost the World Series so narrowly to the Yankees, one of greatest teams ever, should have started the next season full of hope. I remember the same syndrome after Kent finished second in three competitions in 1997: if we all just lifted our games by a mere 5 per cent, we would win not just three competitions but all four! That was the theory at pre-season, anyway.

Now it was the Mets who were 'one more push' away from ultimate glory. I certainly thought so. I might not be an expert, but I had come back from Florida convinced that the Mets would have a good year, possibly even better than the year before. I meant it when I said 'see you at the World Series' as I left the general manager's office. Nor did he seem surprised.

Kent, on the other hand, could scarcely have gone into 2001 a less fancied team. We were still in the first division in both leagues, but only thanks to some miraculous last-minute wins at the end of the previous season. If it had been a struggle then, it could only get harder this year. The first news of the year was that our two strike bowlers, Dean Headley and Julian Thompson, had been forced to retire through injury. There is an old saying in baseball that pitching, not batting, wins pennants. Most people would say the same about cricket. Losing two top-rate bowlers in March is about as bad as it gets.

What about the batsmen? The batsmen were the butt of every journalist's pre-season quip. Chronic underperformers, never-going-to-do-it, overreliant on the overseas star, wasted talent, never knuckled down. *Brittle* was their favourite word. 'A brittle bunch that only managed eighteen batting points in 2000, and no one expects any more this year.' It was the same story in every sports section: nearly every national newspaper's guide to the County Championship predicted we would finish ninth out of nine.

Even a former Kent off spinner who had retired in 2000 and was now working for a spread betting firm, 'opposed' Kent when he set his 'spreads' for the new season. Any money people put on Kent, he thought, was a gift to his firm: so he encouraged them with very generous odds. Not many bit, as the punters say.

If the Mets might jump the final hurdle this time, Kent would fail. Kent were going down, down, down.

And what is the point I am making so subtly here? You guessed it: the Mets were disappointing and Kent came first and third. If that sounds mean, I should add that the first fact, aside from providing the comparative material for this chapter, gave me no pleasure at all. In fact, I was rather looking forward to going back to America and watching the play-offs in October with inside track access. I had even half dreamed of both the Mets and Kent winning in 2001. That would have been a blurb writer's dream. This book's dustjacket could have read something like: 'Two sports; two teams; two titles. One man was there.'

But despite my sending waves of transatlantic wishful thinking to the Mets, it wasn't to be. Not long into the 162-game regular season it became clear that something was badly wrong. Even reading the official website made that clear. By August, I was reading on Mets.com about locker-room bust-ups, factions and ill-discipline, players briefing the media against their colleagues, and the team leader Mike Piazza being ejected from a game (for only the second time in his career) for arguing with an umpire. If their own media guys were hinting at implosion, what were the tabloids saying?

Despite their massive wage bill, the previous season's effort and huge expectations, the Mets fell as far as 14.5 games behind the leaders. Far from qualifying for the World Series, the Mets didn't even make it into the post-season, the all-important knock-out phase that works as an eliminator for the World Series.

Kent, on the other hand, set off to a good start and kept going. It had looked unlikely from the start. The first Championship game of the season was against the County Champions Surrey at the Oval. Surrey had strengthened their already all-star team by signing Mark Ramprakash and Ed Giddins, two of the most successful performers in county cricket over the past five years. Ten out of their eleven had played Test cricket. For us, only Mark Ealham and Min Patel had played Test cricket, as well as our overseas pro Daryll Cullinan – but he hadn't arrived yet from South Africa. As first games go, it didn't look promising.

I was due to bat at number three. Knowing that April wickets tend to favour the ball rather than the bat, I told myself be ready for that early wicket and facing the new ball. And a wicket did come early – early on the second day – as Kent moved to 197 for 1 when Rob Key departed for an untroubled century. I joined Dave Fulton just before he got his ton. What more could I ask for? A flat wicket, a great team platform, an old ball.

Sadly, all I could bring to the party was an undistinguished two, both runs scored through third man. But Matt Walker followed my innings with a punchy hundred of his own. Three hundreds from the first four batsmen, and full batting points against the champions. In 2000, by comparison, we had managed only three Championship hundreds in all sixteen games of the season and had never reached four hundred in any first innings.

But on an obvious level it had still been a bad game for me. We all long to get off to a decent start, to hit the ground running, and the drive from the Oval was a reflective one. But I also thought Kent's batting team had turned a corner. Batting collapses often derive from a kind of perverse and subconscious safety in numbers: a spiralling downwards outlook that might be summed up as 'don't-blame-me-blame-us'.

Now, at least three of us – albeit not me – would be secure in their places and full of confidence. And, as every cricketer will tell you, confidence is half the game. I honestly believed that I would benefit from playing around people who felt an unprecedented sense of belonging and stability. Nor am I rewriting my thoughts with the benefit of hindsight. I wrote just that in a *Times* column after the game.

Later in the season, talking in a bar and celebrating a win, admittedly, but long before the evening degenerated into total farce, a couple of the batsmen told me they had had a quick chat after the Oval game, which had gone so well for them and so badly for me. 'Look after Eddie,' they had said to each other.

That all seemed a long way off going into the second Championship game with a season aggregate of two. I needed some runs. The thought of getting dropped just as we started to bat well was too bleak even to contemplate. I scored nineteen in the first innings against Yorkshire, went down with food poisoning before the third day, cursed my luck, then got a hundred – the best I have played for Kent – batting at number seven in the second innings.

It is amazing how often a slight injury or illness makes people play better. It takes the pressure off, I think, and clears the mind. When you're ill or injured, you haven't got the energy to worry about technique or over-analyse yourself as you play. You just bat. 'Just batting' isn't a bad idea.

Against Pakistan the following week, Key got another hundred. Then at Taunton, Fulton added another; then at Swansea, Walker got his second; at Tunbridge Wells, both Walker and Fulton got hundreds; at Headingley, no one managed three figures for the first time that year, but I got eighty-odd; at Maidstone, Key got ninety and I got a hundred. Including Fulton's hundred against Cambridge at Fenners, the four of us had scored ten hundreds and three nineties in nine first class games, a club record in modern times.

I was much more optimistic about our batting than most during pre-season, but I hadn't even dreamed of a sequence like that. Some of the credit quite rightly went to our new coach, John Inverarity. Wherever he coaches, the team bats better – a pattern repeated too often to be a coincidence. But he strongly denied that he could have been entirely responsible.

The run of form probably had many causes. We certainly played on some good wickets, unlike in the first half of the two previous seasons. And the relentless criticism might have spurred us on a bit (but that's not an invitation for more).

Ironically, I also think the previous four years working very hard with previous coach John Wright had a kind of delayed return in the year after he left.

Those first three tons, I think, broke the spell. The top five ended 2001 with twenty-two first class hundreds: David Fulton contributed nine of those; Matt Walker, Rob Key and myself shared eleven, and Andrew Symonds added two.

We also found an equally unheralded new-ball pairing in Martin Saggers, who notched up more than sixty first class wickets (following his 57 in 2000), and Ben Trott, who fell just short of fifty wickets. Both had been released earlier in their careers; both had reputations to make rather than retain; both bowled very well for long spells during the summer. If I knew more about bowling, I would give them much more space!

A season that had started without a full-time first-team coach – 'How's this Aussie schoolteacher Inverarity going to make any impact at all in only two months?' several people asked me – ended with Kent needing to win the last game to win the Sunday League.

We also needed Leicestershire, who had been runaway leaders for most of the summer, to lose on the same day. After being out in front several times in the past, only to be hauled down, it was nice for Kent to be in the chasing pack for once. The trophy wasn't even in the ground – it was at Nottingham in case Leicester won.

Big games don't come around very often, and when they do everyone, understandably, is desperate to play. When I played in the last game of the 1997 season – which cost us the Sunday League title – I had little idea about how rare it is to get within striking distance of a trophy. This time, I was the one to miss out on selection, and had to watch the game as a helpless observer.

If anything, it's even more draining watching your team rather than playing. You see the pattern of the game unfold but are powerless to change its course. You start to understand how difficult it must be to be a coach.

The first half wasn't too hard to watch, as we racked up 217 off our forty overs – thanks to James Hockley's classy ninety and a quickfire fifty by Rob Key, known better for his technical proficiency against the new ball than for big hitting in the middle order. I will allow myself one slightly pointed comment by saying that his match-winning innings shows the dangers of stereotyping players as either one-day or four-day specialists. Can the two games really be so different?

I was in the strange position of watching the goings-on on the pitch with one eye on the televised game between Leicester and Notts at Trent Bridge. We needed Leicester to lose, of course, to have any chance. But just when it became clear that Notts were on course to do us a favour, we began to lose a grip on our own game. Suddenly the worst case scenario seemed likely: a Leicester defeat *and* a Kent loss. The phrase 'no one to blame but ourselves' loomed uncomfortably. Surely we couldn't be bridesmaids yet again?

We needed something to happen. When Kent are in that situation, we often look to a miserly middle-innings bowling partnership from Mark Ealham and Matthew Fleming. They did it again that Sunday, slowly, almost imperceptibly, applying the pressure and 'squeezing' up the mid-innings run rate. Along with Ian Harvey, they are two of the best one-day bowlers in the country.

But we still needed a brilliant, Bothamesque individual performance from Andrew Symonds to turn the game dramatically in our favour. When he was bowled for seven, trying to hit the ball out of Birmingham, I had a feeling that he might make up for it with something special in the field or with the ball. He did both, taking 5 for 18 then making one of the best run outs I've ever seen.

Before the game we decided not to talk about what was happening at Trent Bridge – if Leicester won it, that was out of our control – while we still had our own game to win. No explicit messages were sent to our players when Notts hit the winning runs, but judging from the way the guys on the field spontaneously celebrated after Matthew Fleming's last ball the news must have leaked out somehow. It was quite a moment.

It was not only Kent's first title for six years, it was also arguably our best all-round season for more than twenty years. I like to think our success in the one-day game owed something to the good form and self-confidence we built up in the longer game – but I would say that, perhaps, having played in every first class game but only a handful of one-dayers. The total package was certainly a happy one: low expectations, good team spirit, lots of runs, a title. We would have settled for that in April.

The next professional sports match I attended was two weeks later at Shea Stadium in New York, where I witnessed the death rites being performed on the Mets' 2001 season.

How different Shea looked from that dramatic final game of the World Series twelve months earlier. A few thousand had turned up out of loyalty or habit – the hardcore fans and the determined hecklers. On a beautiful fall evening, the perfect night for a pennant race thriller, Mets fans forlornly scattered themselves around the 55,000 seater stadium, watching their team lose 10-1 to the Pittsburgh Pirates, one of the worst teams in the league.

There were still probably more Mets fans in that seemingly deserted stadium than there were at Edgbaston for the last day of the Sunday League, but it is a question of atmosphere. There are few bleaker sites than a vast stadium begging for a bigger occasion. Conversely, for cricketers who so often play the last game of the season under the shadow of the new soccer season and with nothing resting on the result, it was a real thrill to see so many Kent fans in Birmingham. They had got up at 6 a.m. to catch the supporters' bus in the hope that Leicester would lose and we would win.

Back at Shea, I viewed the first few innings up in a corporate box, removed from the sounds and smells of the ball park, tempted even to watch it on the in-box widescreen TV. I could see that the Mets had a bad dose of simple error syndrome. Even Mike Piazza, the team leader who had kept doing his bit throughout their slump, muffed an easy play. It is a cruel game in that respect. So much of baseball looks so easy, so slick, so drilled that it serves to highlight the errors. And when the team gets into that catching – or non-catching – downward spiral the opportunities just keep coming to miss the equivalent of open goals. The possibilities for humiliation are endless.

But it was only when I sat down by the dugout, inches away from Bobby Valentine and his team, that I saw the effect of seven months and 162 games of disappointment and thwarted expectations. Amazingly, they had actually won more than eighty games. But even Pittsburgh had won sixty. Even great teams lose a third of their games, and even terrible teams win a third; the Mets simply hadn't won nearly as many of that middle third – the action zone, if you like – as they had anticipated.

Even in a 10-1 defeat there were clean hits, good pitches and great defensive plays. It was the way they were greeted that gave the game away. When something went right, I glimpsed a few players with that 'too little, too late' look; when something went wrong, the expressions switched to 'here we go again'. I guess that had been the pattern for months. Even really strong competitors struggle in that environment: you thought you would be playing big-time ball for the highest prize; instead you are getting whipped by Pittsburgh in a near-deserted home stadium.

Any sportsman would have hated watching those players file away from the dugout to the locker room to face the debriefing, the soul-searching, the finger-pointing, the self-criticism. We have been close enough ourselves, even if not on that scale or on that stage, to imagine the worst. And, in sport, the worst can be pretty bad.

Aside from the spectacle of disappointment, the evening made me think about sport's continual capacity to surprise. Simon Barnes once began a New Year's Day sports column with, 'Want to hear my sporting predictions for the New Year? No, I thought not.' Even the best informed judges can make fools of themselves when it comes to predicting sport, as all those experts who backed the Mets and panned Kent demonstrated.

The signs looked good for the Mets, and their season went nowhere. Kent were written off and battled well. That is not to say the Mets were necessarily weak or culpable; or that Kent heroically defied the odds. The reasons for the Mets' unexpected slump were no more obvious than the factors that went into our comparative good run. A vast number of elements go into producing that curious commodity 'team chemistry'. Even the best planning cannot always get it right – for the simple reason that it is not an exact science.

Perhaps we should be wary in sport of too much simplistic historicism. We didn't work any harder on our batting in 2001, or think about it any more (in fact, we probably thought about it a little less) than we had in any previous season. Our bats were no better; most of us weren't any fitter; we weren't significantly hungrier or more determined to do well.

We are all often guilty, after the result, of assuming things were inevitable, and turning possible explanations into cast-iron facts. In fact, if we remembered all our thoughts – the ones that were proved entirely wrong as much as the ones proved right – we might be more humble in our analysis and more conscious of how difficult sport is to predict. That's one of its joys.

8

11 SEPTEMBER 2001

As if a stuttering and disappointing 162-game regular season were not enough to be worrying about, in mid-September the Mets experienced a new twist of fate, one that nobody could have predicted. In the aftermath of the World Trade Center tragedy of 11 September, the Mets would become the baseball team most closely associated with New York's attempt to recover a sense of celebration and 'normalcy'.

By chance, I was logged on to the internet trying to buy an airline ticket, in part so that I could watch the last part of the Mets' season, when a friend rang me and told me to switch on the TV. 'The World Trade Center has collapsed,' he told me. I replied, no doubt like many other people, 'It couldn't have.'

There is not much left to say either about the two famous skyscrapers or the effect their destruction had on the city's inhabitants. On a more trivial level, I had been grateful many times to the Twin Towers for saving me from taking navigational wrong turns. When you were lost at street level the

Twin Towers often provided a crucial point of reference because you could see them from almost anywhere in Manhattan. The question 'where the hell am I?' was often followed quickly by 'can I see the Twin Towers?'

Even when I wasn't lost, on sunny days I would sometimes sit in Washington Square and look south towards one of the greatest monuments to New York's boundless civic confidence. As the sun moved west in the late afternoon, casting surreal shadows of the Twin Towers across southern Manhattan, I used to feel it would take the most hardened anti-modernist not to enjoy their beauty.

The point has often been made that living in New York in the months and years before 11 September 2001 felt like being in the new Rome. The city inspired a sense of invincibility, the feeling that you could do anything you wanted, and the certainty that you were at the epicentre of the world's trends, ideas and fashions. That sense of being uplifted affected almost everyone who went there.

In one important way, however, sitting in the Windows on the World restaurant on the 107th floor of the World Trade Center was qualitatively different from standing in the Forum in the first century AD. Rome had acquired its centrality and power by conquest. Empires of conquest, no matter how seemingly invincible, are more likely to retain at least a suspicion that one day someone will try to return the military favour. Rome had lived by the sword as an empire – and you don't need me to complete the cliché.

New York, on the other hand, which owed its power and influence not to military might but economic and cultural pre-eminence, luxuriated in a certain innocence. There had been no obvious battle to get all this; why should anyone wish to take it away?

That optimistic spell was broken by the terrorists on 11 September. Even as a non-New Yorker, who has only stayed there for a few months at a time, I felt terribly shaken up. No public disaster has ever affected me in anything approaching the same way. 'How am I going to play cricket tomorrow?' I remember thinking on 11 September.

Fortunately, perhaps, I couldn't watch the whole evolution of the news story on that first day. I had to drive to Manchester to play the last Championship game of the season.

We stood for a minute's silence outside the Old Trafford pavilion just before the start of play on the first day. Because I was due to bat at number three, I was padded up as I stood there on the outfield, hoping all my friends in New York (none of whose phones were working) were okay. Two or three minutes later, when Dave Fulton was out to the fourth ball of the first over, I was walking out to the middle. Taking guard on 12 September was a strange feeling. I was still furious when I got out. 'Today's not a day for throwing tantrums when you're out, Ed,' Min Patel quite rightly told me.

If I was going through all those emotions in Manchester, what must it have been like for a native New Yorker like Al Leiter, the Mets' star pitcher to whom I had talked about cricket back at Spring Training?

Baseball, as it turned out, was suspended for six days after 11 September, but the first major sporting event to take place in the city was the Mets game against their arch-rivals the Atlanta Braves at Shea Stadium. Co-owner Nelson Doubleday and manager Bobby Valentine gave emotional speeches in the clubhouse before the game. During the seventh inning stretch, replacing the normal humalong 'Take Me Out to the Ball Game', Liza Minelli sang 'New York, New York'. That game touched something special in the New York psyche.

In the aftermath of the tragedy, as I read about the Mets' increasing links to the recovery effort in New York, I suspected their season could go in one of two directions. They could either implode completely – 'It wasn't our year all along, and now *this*!' – or they might become inspired.

They became inspired. They won all of their first six games after 11 September, and eight of their first nine. The Miracle Mets were back.

That the Mets found form in such difficult circumstances is perhaps not as surprising as it first might seem. Going through something which dwarfs the problems and anxieties of sport can sometimes release sportsmen from their introspection and fear of failure.

There had been extensive discussion of that syndrome during the Subway Series twelve months earlier. It focused on Orlando Hernandez, the Yankees' Cuban pitcher. Hernandez had acquired a special reputation for the simple reason that he had never lost any game in the post-season. Under pressure, he seemed invincible. Even the 'winningest' (my favourite baseball word) pitcher should expect to lose one game in three. But Hernandez had pitched eight post-season games in his career and won them all.

What did Hernandez have that made him so special? Hernandez claimed that his serenity on the sports field derived from his real-life traumas in Cuba. Hernandez had originally been hailed in his home country as a paragon of Castro's revolution – a living example of Communist triumph. But when he was accused of plotting to defect, Hernandez was summarily banned from playing baseball in Cuba for life.

Instead of accepting his punishment, Hernandez defied the Communist authorities and escaped Castro's regime by undertaking a perilous voyage to America in the bowels of a tiny, leaky fishing boat. Paddling across shark-infested waters to the Land of the Free? As American dreams go, it is a cracker.

Hernandez subsequently said that his astonishing big-match temperament owed much to the dangers of that great escape. 'I wouldn't say I don't get nervous before big games,' he said at one press conference. 'I just know baseball's not life-and-death. I've been there too. If I didn't get scared of those sharks, the opposition batters won't scare me!'

(After all that build-up and psycho-babble, the point of the story, surely, is that Hernandez won Game 3? He lost 4-2, in fact, to the Mets pitcher Ric Reed – who has never, so far as I know, escaped from anywhere on a raft through shark-infested waters.)

But even with an 8-1 post-season record, Hernandez's story is worth telling. Nor is he alone. Many other athletes have flourished after near-death experiences. David Coulthard survived a terrifying plane crash in the middle of the 2000 Formula One season. A few weeks later he won the Monaco Grand Prix, driving, *The Times* reported, 'with an assurance and a level of self-certainty that he had never shown before'.

In the case of the Mets in September 2001, the tragedy was different in that it transcended their personal lives. It was also a civic catastrophe. In such moments the whole role of sport is called into question. The 2001 Ryder Cup, for example, was cancelled – ostensibly because the American team feared the overtly nationalistic nature of the event would be inappropriate; more accurately, perhaps, because they did not consider it safe to travel. The fact that the baseball and football seasons continued demonstrates the extent to which those games are innately bound up with national self-consciousness. Cancelling the Ryder Cup was a shame; cancelling the baseball season would have been surrendering to terror.

The role of sport and entertainment in times of crisis demands difficult judgements. The American chat-show host David Letterman, for example, felt certain he would not be able to put out a show after the World Trade Center tragedy. But shortly after convincing himself that presenting a show such as his would be simply impossible, he came to think that *not* going on air would be a neglect of his civic duty – perhaps even immoral. 'I suddenly felt we had to do it,' he explained, 'more certainly than I have ever felt that about any show.'

Major league baseball was in fact suspended after 11 September, but only for six days. When the Commissioner for Baseball, Bud Selig, announced the resumption of play, he explained, 'I'll be very grateful if we played a small role with other social institutions in helping bring this country back.'

The Mets' first game after the resumption was away at Pittsburgh on 17 September. Following a team meeting before the game, the entire Mets team decided to wear Fire Defence of New York caps instead of the Mets uniform. They were given permission by Major League Baseball to do so for just that game.

Al Leiter, one of the Mets' few native New Yorkers, pitched

the game. 'I just felt a kind of blah feeling of not really being that fired up,' he admitted afterwards. 'I play with so much emotion, fire, anger. I had a tough time.' In his head maybe; not on the mound. Leiter gave up only one run in seven innings, as the Mets won 4-1.

While Leiter had been wondering if he would be able to pitch, manager Bobby Valentine had stayed at Shea Stadium until 3 a.m. the night before the game, directing volunteers who were loading relief supplies for the victims of the tragedy. Shea had become one of the key bases for the rescue work, and Valentine felt a duty to be there. 'It was my diversion. I got into a little project, that was all I did.'

Two nights later, the Mets won again, beating Pittsburgh 9-2. After the victory the team announced that they would play their first game back at Shea without pay. That enabled a donation of $450,000 to be made to the New York Police and Fire Widows and Children Benefit Fund, a charity that had been set up by the former Met Rusty Staub. It gives an indication both of how much baseballers earn and how strongly they felt about the tragedy that Mike Piazza's personal share of the donation was $68,306.

Shea Stadium had to be turned from recovery centre for rescue workers to a baseball field in forty-eight hours. They managed it, and the first major sporting event in New York since the tragedy went ahead on schedule.

The pageantry before the game was part memorial service, part celebration and part pep rally. Diana Ross, supported by fifty-six choristers, belted out 'God Bless America', the Police Department Pipers and Drummers marched from centrefield, and members of the US Marine Corps fired a twenty-one gun salute. It ranks as one of the most extraordinary nights in baseball's recent history.

The Mets did not have permission from Major League Baseball to wear the special FDNY caps that night, but as short stop Rey Ordonez made his way from the clubhouse to the dugout before the game he grabbed his FDNY hat and put it on. The rest of the team did the same. And who was going to stop them?

Despite all the emotion, at 1-2 down in the bottom of the eighth inning, the Mets looked nearly finished. Then Mike Piazza slammed a two-run homer to give the Mets a too-good-to-be-true 3-2 victory. 'I just don't know what to say,' he admitted. Eventually he added, 'We expect to win every game right now, partly because we need to win every game. But also because we're playing completely relaxed, even during what should be the most tense circumstances.'

At the time, Piazza's home run was invested with great hope and considerable meaning. The Mets, in the middle of a screaming streak and riding an emotional high, had still not been eliminated. The old nickname Miracle Mets had found new currency. That hope turned out, we know now, to be illusory. That first week after the resumption of baseball was a beautiful sunset for the Mets, not a brave new dawn. They stumbled fatally in Atlanta the following week, which was asking for one miracle too many.

So much for the illusory hope. But the meaning stays. The Mets did not try to hide behind those emotional days as they reflected on their season. They had not been nearly as good as they should have been for much of the season, and there was no getting away from that fact.

'Explode, Ed!'
Bobby Valentine explains what I have to learn.

CHRIS BOTT

An off-drive trying to be a line-drive.

More comfortable with this one.

Chris Bott

Trying to pull the ball to left field.

A pull for four, but out of bounds in baseball.

'I hit big, I miss big, I like to live as big as I can.'
Babe Ruth

Bradman plays the percentages, Nottingham, 1948.

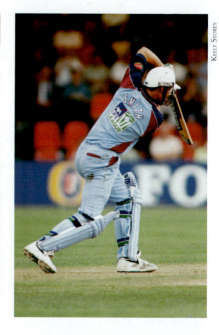

David Fulton
(nine hundreds in 2001).

Me

Rob Key (*above*)
and Matt Walker (*right*)
(four hundreds each in 2001).

But no matter what the prevailing disappointments, they had also been part of something very rare in sport. For a while, the Mets had really mattered. Usually we enjoy sport precisely because it seems to matter so much but carries so little serious baggage. For those days in September, as New Yorkers sought a suitable distraction from their grief and a fitting celebration of their city, baseball meant more than ever. It mattered all the more, in fact, because no one pretended it mattered.

The *New York Times* columnist George Vecsey wrote precisely that in his piece 'The fevered rantings of a Mets fan'. 'All right. I admit it,' he wrote. 'In the middle of August, I said, "Back up the moving van", like Casey Stengel used to say. Zeile out. Ventura out. Ordonez out. Traschel out. Payton out. Wholesale.'

But come late September, even after the Mets had been eliminated, Vecsey decided they had given him something much more important than qualification for the post-season. 'Maybe we didn't make it. But these guys made my season.'

The Yankees may have won the pennant, but the Mets won something else.

9

LAST-MINUTE WINS
AND LOSSES

Kent, thankfully, did not have to deal with the pressure of huge expectation in 2001, nor 11 September, nor the feeling of a 162-game regular season slowly slipping away. But although our season sharply diverged from the Mets' experiences, there were occasional phases of almost spooky coincidence. The closest moment of transatlantic synchronicity came in late July/early August, while Kent were playing Leicestershire and the Mets faced Philadelphia. In both games, the defining moment pitted two former teammates against each other.

It was a big game for Kent. Back in June in the first Championship match between the two teams, Leicester had comprehensively beaten Kent by an innings and 149 runs. That's some margin for a home match played on a flat wicket when you are third in the table. I was in the form of my life yet managed only five and thirty-three. There is never a good time to get a single-figure score, but, as is strangely often the case, I was more disappointed about the thirty-three. The situation demanded a long, patient innings – we needed someone to stick with Dave Fulton – and I did the opposite, scoring a brisk, meaningless thirty-odd.

Nor did it look likely that we would make amends in the return fixture at Leicester. They made around four hundred in both innings, and set us an unlikely target of 401 in just over two sessions, around eighty overs, on the last day. Only once, way back in 1934, had Kent scored more than four hundred in the last innings to win a game.

For most of the day we were just trying to save the game. Winning wasn't even mentioned. The first time winning came into my mind was when I walked off for tea at 200 for 2. Both Andrew Symonds and I had about sixty. 'How many do we need?' he said. 'Only two hundred, right? We can win this.'

To get two hundred in one session you need someone to really go some – in our case, that probably had to be Symmo. He did, smashing 125 off only 134 balls. We still needed ninety-five more when he was out, but the plan was that I would carry on batting normally at the one end. It worked fine until I ran myself out on 107, leaving two new batsmen at the crease and all three results – a Kent win, a draw, and now a Leicester win, too – possible again.

On days like that, potentially special days, it is only when you are out that you realise the extent of your emotional involvement. For three or four hours you have been in the thick of it – weighing up risks, taking chances, wondering if it might be your day, trying not to get too far ahead of yourself – and then it is over. For you anyway. All you can do then is watch. Having been one of the most important players in this particular game, you are suddenly one of the least important. You did not finish the job; and you can only hope someone else does.

I didn't even get out of my kit. I just sat there padded up watching us creep towards the target. Another ten runs, one cleanly-struck boundary, another wicket, another new batsman – on it went, the balance constantly shifting, but looking increasingly like it wouldn't be our day.

Usually I am an optimist in run chases. But with 14 needed off the last over, I was braced for one of the biggest lows of my career. Because when you fail having created an unlikely chance for yourself – like the Mets' did in late September – it hurts double.

The batters were Paul Nixon, on 13, and Martin Saggers, who had two. Nixon got two off the first ball – 12 off five.

Then another two. *Ten off four, what a difference just one big hit would make . . .*

Then another two. *Okay, do it in twos if you must.*

Two more. *Six off two. We are starting to believe again . . .*

FOUR! *I hit the ceiling. For the first time in about an hour, we are favourites.*

So just two off the last would do. I am now leaning over the balcony, ready to jump.

SIX!

I have never seen a dressing room like it. Admittedly, I haven't played in many games that we won off the last ball. But who has? It is a magical feeling, release as much as elation. That sounds bad in a way, because 'release' suggests being saved from a negative experience. But that's how it felt. I just couldn't face the thought of coming that far and then not winning it. They later decided that the 'six', though it comfortably cleared the outfielder, did not clear the rope, and was in fact four. But it was more than good enough.

Moments like that – running on to the outfield to hug someone who has just won a game off the last ball – make sport seem entirely worthwhile. All cricketers have plenty of muted days: long sessions in the field, failures with the bat, luckless bowling spells, boring draws. You quickly forget those days in the glow of that kind of win. One-day cricket, of course, offers the best chance of a thrilling finish. Perhaps that is why winning a close Championship encounter is sometimes even more enjoyable. They don't come around very often, and are all the sweeter for it.

Some of the thrill stems from the sheer improbability. What odds would you get that a four-day game (that is twenty-five and a half hours and 400 overs of cricket) would end up with two runs needed off the last ball?

For me, one of the joys of the experience was completely losing myself. That is an easy thing to say, but not so easy to do. How often, if we are being truthful, do we live entirely in the present, not worrying at all about the future, or reassessing the past? That feeling – being there, now, and so very happy – is not peculiar to sport. But for many of us sport offers one of the best ways of getting there.

I will never forget watching Nico hit that ball, or the moment during its trajectory (when it was somewhere over mid-wicket's head, I think) that I realised he had hit it well enough, or the second I saw it land and became convinced that we really had won, or the thrill of that sprint out to the pitch. They are indelible memories.

Perhaps it was always going to be that kind of game. An

astonishing 1583 runs were scored in the match and seven different players scored hundreds. But the statistics are nothing compared to the ironies. How about this for a sequence? Trevor Ward dropped Matt Walker, who went on to get a hundred; I dropped Trevor Ward, who then completed a ton against his old team; Paul Nixon dropped Darren Maddy, who then converted his first hundred of the year; then Paul Nixon hit Darren Maddy's last ball for four to win the match. 'Go figure', as they say in America.

But the most ironic part of the story – and this is where the parallel with the Mets comes in – is that the man who hit the winning runs had done as much as anyone to build the team he was playing against. As a Leicester player, Paul Nixon had been at the centre of the team spirit and work ethic that helped to make them County Champions two years out of three. By moving to Kent after a decade at Grace Road, he left behind the friends and colleagues that he had played with all through his professional career.

In Nico's first year at Kent, we lost three games and drew one against Leicester. In 2001, we lost the first two. When you are trying to convince yourself that you have done the right thing, losing five of the first six games against your old county cannot be easy.

Sporting motivation is too complex to explain glibly. But a sense of balancing the ledger, of making it all seem worthwhile, of getting a return on an investment – all those feelings probably contributed to Nico being particularly keen to get that fourteen off the last over against his old colleagues. The way he furiously kicked down the stumps in celebration immediately afterwards certainly showed *something* being released!

It is also a reminder about how unsentimental sport can be. The person who bowled the last over was Darren Maddy, one of his closest friends at Leicester. The two of them had spent seven or eight years helping each other. Now they found themselves in a duel of sorts. To some extent, it often happens in sport – such as when England players come up against each other in county cricket. But that is slightly different. They were opponents before they were colleagues, rather than vice versa as in the case of Maddy and Nixon.

Somehow, in the jumble of emotions they must both have been experiencing, they had to clear their minds and *just do their job*. Bowl it straight, watch the ball, whatever it might be. There was no room for empathy or abstract thinking. *Just do the job.*

It might not be easy for cricketers who move counties when they play their old team-mates, but at least cricketers largely get to choose whether they change teams. If they want to stay put, and their employers continue to offer them a job, there is little risk of upheaval. There is no transfer system to speak of in cricket. If a player becomes a free agent, or falls out with his county, he might consider a move. But he cannot be transferred against his will. Cricketers might not get the cash; but nor do we get the uncertainty.

Baseball could not be more different. The players are not only people, with careers and families, but also financial assets, units of worth. Relatively early in baseball history, in the 1930s, the legendary manager and owner Connie Mack used to build a championship team and then promptly sell it for the cash. It was a game, sure, and you tried to win;

but it was a business, too, and making money was even better.

One way to interpret baseball history is as an ongoing struggle between the players and the owners. Baseball has been a proper professional game ever since the late nineteenth century; but being a proper professional game has not always meant the players were treated as proper professionals. The most infamous example was the so-called 'gentleman's agreement' between all the baseball owners that banned African-Americans from every playing in the major leagues. It lasted until 1947, when Branch Rickey invited Jackie Robinson to play for the Brooklyn Dodgers.

Scarcely less important than the 'gentleman's agreement' was the 'reserve clause'. The clause demanded that all major league baseball professionals had to play for their existing team unless the owner was prepared to release them to play elsewhere. In practical terms, that gave the players only one real bargaining power. If they wanted more money or better terms they were forced to say to the owner: either you give me what I want, or else I stop playing baseball. Going elsewhere was not an option. Considering that most baseballers were uneducated farm hands and blue-collar workers, it was easier to walk out of baseball than to walk into employment in another career. Countless players 'held out'; not many stayed out.

All that changed in the 1970s when the players' union hired the brilliant trade unionist Marvin Miller as their spokesman. Miller was not afraid to stand up to the owners; better still, he tended to win. By turning players into free agents he also turned many of them into millionaires. Miller was a formidable example of the species *homo economicus*.

To say it has worked out well for the players is an under-statement. In 1966 the salaries of all major league players totalled $9.5 million. Today, many teams boast at least one player (and often several) who alone earns more than that in one season. Baseball now boasts a highly disproportionate number of the best paid sportsmen in the world. In recent years, the tag 'world's highest paid athlete' – excluding endorsements – has been passed from baseball player to base-ball player. At the time of writing, it resides with Alex Rodriguez of the Texas Rangers, who is guaranteed to earn not less than $20 million over the next ten years. 'You do the math', as Americans say.

Despite the huge advantages contemporary baseball players now have over their predecessors, in one crucial regard they are in the same boat. They can still be traded. In *Ball Four*, Jim Bouton wrote memorably about the upheaval of waking up one morning and discovering you play for a different team.

The worst case scenario is that you have been dropped to the minors. The glamour of the big leagues will soon be replaced by the anonymity of the 'prospects' and the has-beens. Being dropped to the minors is like being dropped to the second team in county cricket – which is quite bad enough – with the added disincentives that the minor league team probably operates in a different state, with dif-ferent players and new coaches. You might not have met any of them before. You could be shunted from New York to California, or from Florida to Washington state. No wonder Jim Bouton referred to being moved to the minors as 'dying':

April 14

I died tonight.

I got sent to Vancouver.

My first reaction: outrage.

My second reaction: Omigod! How am I going to tell Bobbie? The *problems*. Where to live? How to get rid of the place we'd already signed a lease on in Seattle? What would happen to the $650 deposit? Moving again. *Again.* And we just got here . . .

. . . I said to the CEO, 'Well, if I do real good down there, I'd like to come back.'

I expected him to say, 'Of course. You do good down there and we'll yank you right back here, stick you in and you'll win the pennant for us.' Or something reassuring like that. Instead he said, 'Well, if you do good down there, there's a lot of teams that need pitchers.'

Good grief. If I ever heard a see you later, that was it.

But Bouton's case was extreme. More often you remain part of the club's thinking even if you have been dropped to the minors. It might only be a temporary death.

Ironically, that cannot be the case if you are traded to the majors. Then it really is all over for you as a Yankee or a Met or whatever. You went to bed hoping your team was going to win the pennant; you wake up and have to force yourself to hope that its arch-rival is going to win.

Experiences like that make the mixed emotions of playing against a county you choose to leave look comparatively moderate.

I couldn't help thinking about the harsh business of trading as I watched general manager Steve Philips make mid-season personnel changes in an attempt to prevent the Mets sliding further down the National League East. If you need new players, unless you can find top-class players from nowhere – and not many people can – you have to trade. That can mean extreme measures. If the team can't score enough runs, perhaps a top pitcher, even if he has done nothing wrong, has to go. If the team is perceived to be a long way from contention, it might even be prudent to trade two or three veteran players at the top of their games for several younger 'prospects'. Trading is gambling with people.

The Mets took some tough decisions about personnel in mid-season 2001. None can have been harder than the decision to trade Turk Wendell, Dennis Cook and Todd Pratt. Cook's case was a little different from that of the other two – he was an experienced 'tradee', who would be a free agent at the end of the season anyway. For Pratt and Wendell the moves were probably more wrenching. They were people who had been central to the Mets enterprise, not just the Mets franchise.

Wendell was traded on 28 July. On 29 July he had to play for his new team. The game was at Shea Stadium against the Mets. When he arrived at the ball park before play, by habit Wendell drove into the Mets' players' car park. At the players' entrance, he had to check himself before turning left into the visitors' locker room, not right into the home clubhouse – as he had done every time he had been to Shea in the previous four years. He even wore a pair of Mets shorts to warm up in because he hadn't yet been issued with all his Philadelphia kit.

Wendell is a 'set up man'. That means it is his job to restrict the opposition scoring after the starting pitcher has finished his six or seven innings, and before the 'finisher' pitches the ninth. When Wendell took to the mound at Shea that day he was given an appreciative cheer by his old fans. 'I tried not to listen,' he said subsequently, 'I didn't want to get caught up in the emotion. I had a job to do. I did it in the eighth.'

The problem came in the ninth. Having not given up a single run in the eighth, at the bottom of the ninth Wendell served up a 'sinker' to Mets hitter Robin Ventura that, in the pitcher's own words, 'never sank'. Instead Ventura hit a home run over the rightfield wall to turn a 3-3 tie into a 4-3 Mets win.

Wendell never saw the pile of jubilant Mets at home plate waiting for Ventura because, as he said, 'I didn't look.'

'You give up the home run, turn around and see the ball go over the fence,' Wendell said. 'For a second there, I was like, "why me?" This probably takes the cake in terms of being in strange situations in baseball.' Moving jobs is one thing; starting a new job in your old office is a bit much.

Wendell was having the converse experience at Shea that Paul Nixon had gone through at Grace Road. It could have gone either way for both of them. As it turned out, Nixon had one of his best days, Wendell his worst.

Aside from the coincidence of being hit for a home run by a former colleague in the same week that Paul Nixon hit a four off Darren Maddy, there is another reason for mentioning Wendell. He is famously superstitious. For fear of being 'outed' myself as a sufferer from superstition, I should add that I share the trait.

In Wendell's case, his superstition takes the form of numbers and rituals. He signed a three-year contract for $9,999,999.99 (before you write to complain about sporting salaries, I promise there is a decimal point in there somewhere), and he wears, inevitably, number ninety-nine on his shirt.

His more famous superstition involves the rosin bag which pitchers position behind the pitching mound. They will often pick up the bag and toss it from hand to hand to get a better grip on the ball. Wendell doesn't just pick it up; he picks it up then slams it with a great flourish back down into the dirt. 'I have thrown down the rosin bag', he implies. 'Now I am ready to throw the baseball.'

The fans love it. Even the Mets fans, torn between supporting their old favourite and their team, gave him a special cheer when he threw down the rosin bag that day in late July. It is a crazy ritual, really, but pitchers *are* crazy. Who wouldn't be, considering the pressure they are under? One hit given up and it could be game over.

All cricket batsmen – in many ways analogous, as I have suggested, to pitchers – will understand. The pitcher, like the batsman, is the constant. For that reason, I think, visible signs of superstition are more common among pitchers and cricket batsmen. They have more time on their hands, less chance of recovering from a disastrous error, and, perhaps, more to worry about. In the lengthy pauses between plays, the zoom lens is more often on them.

Why do we bother with superstition? I have several recurrent superstitions. When I asked one umpire how many balls were left in the over – for the fiftieth time that day, as always after three balls had been bowled – he understandably quipped, 'That superstition can't help all that much, Ed – I see you are still getting out these days!' He had a point.

But superstition is perhaps the wrong word for the series of things I do between each ball. It is more a routine. A slight walk away from the crease, putting the toe of the bat down on the ground in the same way, saying the same things to myself every time, tapping the bat in the same way as the bowler walks back to his mark.

I'm not thinking: 'If I miss out a step of my routine I will get out.' I'm not thinking much at all when it's working well because I am engaged with a process that distracts me from thinking about getting out. Of course, it doesn't always work – as that umpire rightly pointed out. But it usually helps. I think.

It is also habit, of course, and sometimes it doesn't do any harm to streamline such habits. In fact, I am much less 'superstitious' than I used to be. But I think having some kind of routine is a good thing for me. It's everyone else it drives crazy. Quite often I see my team-mate batting at the other end explain to the umpire why I keep asking for guard or the number of balls left. I trust they are putting my side of the story!

That's the best defence I can give. But I am not even going to try to justify why I adjust the Velcro on my pads countless times before I bat. One day I must have started doing it and it simply stuck. Perhaps it is a ritualistic way of beginning the preparation for my innings. Perhaps it makes perfect sense. Perhaps it is the future of batsmanship? Or perhaps some things are just beyond rationality.

But irrationality and chance – like the spectacle of Turk

Wendell throwing down the rosin bag, or the coincidence that two batters, one playing for Kent and one for the Mets, should hit game-winning blows off ex-colleagues in the same week of the season – are two of the enduring fascinations of sport.

So much for Maddy, Nixon, Wendell and Smith. What happened to Robin Ventura? At Spring Training, he was introduced to me as 'one of the nicest men in baseball' and everyone seemed to anticipate him improving on a disappointing 2000 season. He didn't. That game-winning home run against Turk Wendell was a stand-out moment, not the norm.

In the newspaper postmortems that followed the Mets' failure to reach the post-season, Ventura, if he could bear to look, would have read speculation that his time was up with the Mets. 'Beginning June 13,' I read in *Newsday*, 'Ventura batted only .193, with a .332 slugging average and committed 15 of his 16 errors. But will the Mets manage to persuade another club to pick up his $8.5 million wage bill?' That's the downside of the $8.5 million.

10

BOGEY TEAMS
AND DYNASTIES

So what did happen to stop the Mets' glorious post-11 September winning streak? Answer: Atlanta.

Most sides, whatever the sport, have a bogey team. No matter how good the team's form, or how well they are playing, or how high their confidence – it all tends to wobble when they play their bogey team. With each loss, especially losses that really ought to have been wins, the syndrome deepens, and the bogey looms larger.

The Mets' bogey team is the Atlanta Braves. Even at Spring Training, the Braves cropped up in conversation more often than any other club. Several people said to me, 'Well, the Braves have certainly been massive for us in the past' – meaning a massive threat, a massive challenge, massively important.

Inevitably, 2001 all came down to the Braves again. On 23 September – having won eight of their last nine games – the Mets played Atlanta at Shea Stadium. The equation was simple: having started the season so badly, there was no margin for error now. The streak had to run and run. 'I wouldn't say we ever look forward to playing the Braves,' Bobby Valentine said at the time, 'but we're really up for this one.'

For much of the game, it all went according to plan. 4-1 up going into the ninth inning, the Mets threw the ball to Armando Benitez, their much discussed 'closer'. It was Benitez's job to kill off the opposition. A closer doesn't have to pitch for many innings, perhaps only one or one and a half. That might only be a handful of pitches. But considering the stage of the game, they have to be good pitches.

Closers, in baseball lingo, usually 'throw smoke'. With no reason to leave anything in the tank, they tend to throw mainly overpowering fast balls. Even among flame-throwing closers, Benitez has an impressive armoury of fast balls and variations. He 'saved' forty-three games in 2001, the most in the league.

Despite his formidable talent and raw materials, Benitez has tended to have difficulties in big games. He came to the Mets with that reputation and he hasn't shaken it off. In Game 1 of the Subway Series in 2000, he gave up a lead that cost the Mets the game. At Spring Training, several people suggested that Benitez would soon turn round that reputation for 'not stepping up', just as Piazza had done the previous year. 'He has a 97 m.p.h. fast ball, a change-up, and . . .'

With all that up his sleeve, even against the Atlanta Braves surely Benitez couldn't give up three or more runs in less than one inning at Shea Stadium? He did. He pitched two-thirds of an innings, thirty-three pitches in all, and gave up three runs – all of them home runs. Having been allowed to get back into it at 4-4, Atlanta went on to win 5-4 in the eleventh innings. The Braves bogey had struck again.

Worse was to follow. Mathematically, the Mets could still get away with that one loss and make it into the post-season. But now there really was absolutely no margin for error. Wins were essential. On 29 September, this time at Turner Field (named after the club's owner Ted Turner, the TV mogul) in Atlanta, the Mets again went into the ninth with an apparently impregnable lead.

Leiter had pitched brilliantly again, giving up one run in eight innings. When the pitching coach came out to the mound to tell him he was being replaced, Leiter retorted, 'What use is eight innings?' But Benitez had already been called upon to 'close' another match. Again he gave up three home runs in two-thirds of an inning, and five runs in all.

It was one meltdown too many for the Mets. This time their season was over barring a succession of statistical freaks. The Braves had done for them again.

It is a moot point whether Benitez would ever have given up those ninth inning runs against a normal team, one which had no special baggage for the Mets. We can never be sure if or at what point he got that fatal 'here-we-go-again' feeling. Maybe he just pitched normally and was unlucky. Luck, chance, fate – call it what you will – the Braves had come round on the game schedule at two crucial moments, and the Mets had failed to overcome their nemesis.

For many years Kent's bogey team was Warwickshire. It always seemed to be Warwickshire. Of all the Kent games I ever watched, I best remember a semi-final at Edgbaston. Warwickshire were also in the middle of their glory years:

with Dermot Reeve as captain and Bob Woolmer as coach, they just kept winning trophies – championships, miraculous one-day finals, one-day leagues. If it was silver, they won it. Kent at that time had a very good team but hadn't won anything for twelve years. A semi-final away draw at Edgbaston was a challenging throw of the dice.

NatWest Trophy matches in those days were sixty (not fifty) overs per side. That leaves a lot of time for normal batting, and on flat wickets seriously high scoring was often possible. You could get 280 without smashing the ball from the first over. So when Warwickshire set Kent 266 it was not remotely disastrous. When I met up with Graham Cowdrey for a minute between innings outside the pavilion to thank him for getting me a ticket, he simply said, 'I think we'll get them.'

It looked as though we would. Trevor Ward got one of his effortless five-an-over-from-the-start eighties – the type of innings you don't realise is that difficult until you see everyone else try. When Neil Taylor crafted a well-paced sixty, the match was there for the taking. But after a double breakthrough, and with two new batsmen at the crease, Dermot Reeve brought up his fielders. 'You can't win it in ones and twos,' he was saying, 'you'll have to hit over the top.' The stranglehold was effective and Kent collapsed. Brilliant bowling, brave captaincy, tumbling wickets, game lost.

My dad and I were seated in the middle of a group of Warwickshire fans whose favourite player was the Warwickshire all-rounder Paul Smith. 'Come on Smithy son', I heard a thousand times in broadest Brummy. 'Shatter 'is stumps!'

Anything but bowled, I thought. Anything but bowled.
Bowled. 'Attaboy, Smithy son, you shattered 'is stumps!'
Get me out of here.

Of all sporting phenomena, the batting collapse is one of
the most graphic expressions of group self-doubt. Sometimes,
of course, it isn't self-doubt. It is just one of those days, when
they bowl jaffas, or you nick everything and miss nothing.
That isn't just a batsman making excuses. I really believe that
not all bad days are worthy of too much analysis. But more
often, a collapse tends to be the gruesome result of a lack of
belief. The point being that bogey teams trigger the first
symptoms of that lack of belief earlier than other teams. That
terrible thought, the thought we all have to fight when wickets start to go – 'here we go again' – comes earlier and strikes
deeper. Because we *have* been there before.

Once again, we see how the equivalent of losing wickets in
cricket is giving up runs in baseball. Meltdown in baseball is
conceding a series of home runs; meltdown in cricket is the
batting collapse. Either way, it is a terrible feeling.

Bogeys have to be conquered some time. So when Kent
played Warwickshire at Edgbaston in the last game of the
2001 Sunday League, I hoped this would be the moment. A
Kent win, a Leicester loss – you know the story by now . . .

We had been in a similar situation at the end of 1995, just
over a year after that NatWest defeat at Edgbaston. Going
into the last game of the season, Kent would definitely win
the Sunday League if either they won or their closest rival
lost. The match, inevitably, was against Warwickshire.

Kent lost; but so too did the second-placed team – so Kent

were champions. Some mean-spirited supporters/detractors claimed they might as well not have won the league, given that they lost the 'decider' that ended up not being a decider. 'It's a league, right?' one of the Kent players later reassured me. 'In a league, it's the guys with the most points, not the team who wins on the last day, who gets the trophy.' He was completely right, but it also would have been nice to have won. Especially against . . .

Six years later, we are back at Edgbaston, this time with an almost completely different team. Of that 1995 team, only Matthew Fleming, Mark Ealham, Min Patel, Dave Fulton and Matt Walker are still around. But we started to make the odd unforced mistake, wobbled a little bit – it couldn't happen again, could it? It didn't this time, as we all know. And finally, for the first time since the early 1980s, Kent *won a match to win a trophy*.

Bogey teams also sometimes reverse roles with their victims. When I was growing up, Kent always seemed to lose to Essex. Fletcher, Gooch, Lever, Hardie – they always got there in the end, often off the last ball it seemed, whether the match was at Chelmsford or Canterbury. 'Essex next week, then' we would say, having seen the programme. 'Oh dear.' The drive back from a Sunday League match against Essex was usually an unhappy one. Even now when we play Essex I still think of them as a great club – largely because their era of dominance in the County Championship coincided with the period of my most obsessive fanship. Those three red Essex cutlasses were dangerous weapons.

So I was amazed when someone told me that we have beaten Essex in our last five first class games, three times by an innings. I played in nearly all those wins; I even hit the winning runs in at least one game, so it's not as though I wasn't around to see the reversal. Kent vs Essex: who'd have guessed it?

One day that reversal will happen between the Mets and the Atlanta Braves. Soon, I hope. One day, in all probability, but hopefully not so soon, Kent will start losing to Essex again. It is the nature of bogey teams.

Very occasionally you get to become everyone's bogey team. You inspire that feeling of inferiority in every opponent, not just one team which you have traditionally beaten. The name of the other lot scarcely matters. It must be a nice feeling. You are a dynasty.

I have watched several dynasties. Liverpool in the eighties; Bath rugby union club in the late eighties and early nineties; Warwickshire in the mid-nineties; Manchester United from the mid-nineties onwards; the Yankees at the turn of the century; Australia in recent years. Those teams became synonymous with success in their sport. More than success; it felt like *inevitable* success. That requires a structure and a system, a leader and usually a spirit.

The Arsenal team of the nineties, that so often used to beat teams far more talented than themselves, talked about 'the Arsenal spirit'. You saw it in the way they defended: with complete trust, commitment, never just hoping that someone else would take responsibility. If they had been in an American sports franchise, Adams, Bould, Keown, Winterburn and Dixon would have been much more celebrated much earlier – 'the mean machine' maybe. It wouldn't have taken ten years for people to have realised the goals weren't going in too much at one end.

The Yankees, it has become very clear to me every time I have seen them play, are a dynasty *par excellence*. When they win, it seems inevitable; when they are losing, even near the death, it seems only temporary; they don't panic – they've been there before and got out of the jam. Even when they are being outplayed (rare in itself) you would never bet against them. Having seen so many impossible comebacks in the past, you always have the suspicion they might do it again.

Maybe that is the point. Perhaps the opposition have that feeling too. At several stages of the 2001 season the Yankees were all but finished. It doesn't get more serious than being 2-0 down (with two away games coming up) in a best of five series, as the Yankees were against Oakland Athletics in the first round of the play-offs.

But then strange things started to happen. Veterans found last moments of inspiration, rookies stepped on to the big stage, the Yankees turned up the heat, and the As started to look like the Yankees were their bogey team. And, just like a team playing a familiar nemesis, self-belief quickly turned to disbelief. We had this won, you could see written on As' faces, but I suppose it *is* the Yankees. There is nothing so damaging in sport – or so self-fulfilling – as that here-we-go-again feeling.

And there they did go again, out to the Yankees. Not that the Yankees particularly *are* a bogey team for Oakland. That is to say, the Yankees are everyone's bogey team, not just Oakland's. They have the wood on everyone. That is what a dynasty is.

A test of a dynasty is not only how many titles it wins. It is how it wins those titles. And whether it looks likely to keep on winning them.

Money is a big help. The Yankees are drowning in money. The NY branded baseball cap – as worn by David Beckham, even before the Yankees and Manchester United joined forces – is one of the marketing success stories of all time. Every sale helps, and, boy, do baseball clubs need the cash. Even when they won the World Series in 2000, the Yankees immediately strengthened their roster at huge expense by signing Mike Mussina, the best available free agent pitcher. Now that's the kind of owner most managers would kill for.

But as even a glance at the table of richest franchises reveals, there is no guaranteed correlation between money and performance. Several baseball clubs are stinking rich and play stinking baseball. Being a rich club is like being an expensive dresser. Money guarantees expensive individual garments, but it will not guarantee the items don't clash. There's nothing uglier than tasteless expense. So it is with sports franchises. In some ways, a rich club full of strong personalities creates new potential for complete disaster. There is no escaping the need for good judgement if you are to get the chemistry right.

Recently the Yankees have got the chemistry right in a way they didn't before. They were just as rich in the past; just not as good. George Will once argued that the Yankees would never be a winning team because their owner George Steinbrenner believed he could buy success. Will was half right. But once they had the right formula for success, the money certainly helped.

So you have to tip your hat to Joe Torre's management and

his players. But not many outside the Yankees fan club will. Being hated by everyone else can be seen as another defining characteristic of being a dynasty. Even a relative baseball novice like me found it hard to enjoy watching the Yankees win. As a nascent Mets fan I couldn't get beyond seeing the Yankees as the vanquishers of the Mets in the previous year's World Series.

My rational side fought such a blinkered response. It was even in my own interests to root for the Yankees. Because I was based in New York while I finished this book, a Yankees win was great material. It kept the whole topic in general conversation and at the forefront of the media. I would turn on the television saying to myself, 'I hope the Yankees are winning', then sigh with disappointment when they were. As logic goes, that is at the same level as randomly singing 'We all hate Man U' on the terraces.

But logic goes out of the window where dynasties are concerned. The cuts are too deep. I once met a salesman who is a Mets fan. 'The more I hate the Yankees,' he said, 'the more they win.' Try not hating them, then? 'That's what my missus says, man. It's logical, I know, and I do try, but I just can't help it. I hate those damned Yankees!'

In truth that is the highest compliment of all. Dynasty hatred is the simplest form of hate: pure envy. Because no matter what we may say about underdogs, bigger pictures and not-just-the-winning, deep down we all know how much fun being a dynasty must be.

There are countless sports legends about what it is like playing in a dynasty. Walking through the tunnel at Anfield, putting on the All Black jersey, wearing the Yankee pinstripe.

Dynasties have their own symbols, and those symbols matter. For that reason, perhaps, a too highly developed sense of irony works against creating that kind of dynasty.

But the best piece I ever read about the chemistry of success wasn't about a dynasty *per se* – though it could have been – but about an individual performer. But the principle is the same. Having lifted and adapted so many of his ideas, this time I am going to quote Simon Barnes's actual words. They deserve it.

It's five years ago this weekend that Frankie Dettori rode all seven winners at the British Festival of Racing at Ascot and established a sporting legend. 'I am just warming up,' said Dettori afterwards. 'Is there any more racing?'

We can allow genius to take its course for the first six races. But the seventh? Dettori rode Fujiyama Crest, a 12-1 chance when the betting shops opened for business that day. Dettori won and threw the entire bookmaking industry into pandemonium, with jockey-struck mug punters collecting at odds of 25,095-1 . . .

Sports psychologists talk about a winner's confidence that can 'radiate like an aura and be a palpable threat to every competitor'. Graham Sharpe [a racing writer] favours a kind of collective hysteria, along the lines of UFO sightings, or involuntary peer pressure.

It's one of those sporting conundrums in which just about everybody has a piece of the answer: Dettori's brilliance, the debilitating effect this had on his opponents, their reluctance to spoil a beautiful story.

My own contribution to the debate concerns the galvanising communication between horse and rider. It is the exact corollary of the truth that horses know when the rider is nervous.

Fujiyama Crest certainly sensed Dettori's supreme confidence, and if that sort of thing doesn't affect a horse's performance, then I've never patted a horse in my life. 'He'd have won on a seaside donkey in the last', said former champion jockey, John Francome.

We've all had that Frankie experience – even if it lasts only for ten minutes. They don't come very often, but at least in sport we can experience them vicariously.

Now there are no horses in sports like cricket and baseball. But there are team-mates. They, too, and just as subconsciously, sense the confidence of those around them. They, too, are lifted by colleagues with real belief. They, too, are affected by the prevailing tone of the day. We are all human, in other words. Not least the opposition, who are hit by the negative force of that infectious self-belief. Because that is what dynasties have: infectious self-belief. It starts somewhere, in the core of the team perhaps, but it infiltrates everyone. It is difficult to beat and fascinating to watch.

11

THE NUMBERS GAME

One of sport's enduring fascinations is its ability to fulfil the natural human impulse to seek rational criteria of quality. What other sphere of excellence is as easy to measure as sport? Which painter, composer, novelist or pop star was the greatest? You say Raphael, I say Rembrandt; you say Bach, I say Wagner; you say Tolstoy, I say George Eliot; you say Elvis, I say Bob Dylan. It might be amusing for a few minutes, but we quickly run out of objective means of judgement. Most people can agree on Shakespeare, but not much else.

Sport, on the other hand, though it might be the toyshop of the adult world, certainly rewards comparative analysis more richly than other more 'serious' subjects. Admittedly, the desire to rank one's sporting heroes might not be very grown up. It is probably no coincidence that when I moved into my teenage years, and socialising started to take over, I stopped memorising the Kent averages. The same emotional deficiency that leads people to line up their records in alphabetical order, Nick Hornby wrote in *Fever Pitch*, turns them into sporting obsessives. Hornby added that he didn't know many women with alphabetically catalogued record collections.

Some sports appeal to budding cataloguers more than others. Ironically, football is not one of them. It is so fluid and low-scoring that its statistics do not easily represent on-field influence. You can't score goals, of course, without people to create them. And even the 'Beckham vs Vieira – passes completed' percentiles of today's Sky Sports Premiership coverage don't always match up with the game as I experienced it.

Even the statistics in rugby union, a game of territory and possession, can be unconvincing. The most repeated stat is points per game. England's Jonnie Wilkinson might average fourteen points; and Wales's Neil Jenkins eleven. But that wouldn't explain that Wilkinson, playing for a dominant England side, gets many more kickable conversions than Jenkins, who has lived off scraps in a struggling Welsh team for much of his career.

Cricket and baseball, perhaps more than any games, offer the fans statistical nourishment. All cricket fans know Bradman averaged ninety-nine in Test cricket. All baseball fans know that Ted Williams hit .406 in 1941. Do all football fans know how many goals Gary Lineker, or Bobby Charlton, scored for England? Do rugby fans know how many tries John Kirwin scored for the All Blacks? I doubt it. So what is it about bat and ball games? Why do they inspire such absurdly knowledgeable and analytical fans?

As a nine-year-old I would often fall asleep with the bedside light on and the *Playfair Cricket Annual* wedged open at the Kent averages page. I was that kind of fan. For me, cricket – as the sports psychologists would now say about winning – wasn't a sometimes thing, it was an all-the-time thing.

At every Kent home Sunday League game, both my sister and I used separately to keep track of each run, over and dismissal on our printed scorecards. She always filled in her scorecard much more neatly and accurately than I did, which drove me mad. I haven't forgotten much from those days. Even now, I could tell anyone off the top of my head what Chris Cowdrey averaged when he had his best year with the bat (fifty-six in 1983), the most number of wickets Chris Penn took in a season (eighty-one in 1988), and the intimate details of the Lord's finals that I went to in 1984 and 1986. Kent lost to Middlesex on the last ball on each occasion (Ellison bowled to Emburey in 1984, Hughes to Dilley in 1986), Chris Cowdrey scored fifty-eight for Kent in 1984 and Graham Cowdrey fifty-eight in 1986.

I'm not even trying yet. Those numbers are to me what rhyming poems were to my grandfather – memories that don't fade. I know them better than my own statistics – and I've only been playing for a few seasons.

Some of my friends took the statistical quest to a far deeper level than I did. I knew people at school who seemed to have swallowed *Wisden*. It didn't matter to them if they could play cricket or not. In fact, the real 'statos' tended to be very bad leg spinners who subsequently turned their talents to devising new methods of scoring cricket matches in multicoloured pencils. Learning cricket statistics – you didn't set out to learn them, of course, you just read them and, unlike homework, they stuck – was an end in itself, unrelated to your own talent as a player, a strange but enduring world of private fantasies and recurring numbers.

Averages and idiosyncratic statistics have long been part of cricket's mythical appeal, so much so that the yellow-covered *Wisden* – which still records some schoolboy averages – exerts an almost biblical hold on its many disciples. Cricket offers the serious fan more than a team to support and players to admire; it brings them a form of companionship, a kind of belonging, and a mental challenge. Such fans seek desperately to understand cricket, to master its nuances from the sidelines even if they never could in the middle.

But baseball fans make cricket obsessives look positively casual. The game itself, it must be admitted, is still more suited to precise scientific study. Not just runs but hits make it into the score book; fielding errors, thanks to fielding gloves, are so infrequent that they are part of the official scoring system; and pitchers have their careers summarised in a boxing-style ratio of games won against games lost.

Baseball, in fact, is a stats junkie's heaven. Even I – someone who once memorised now long-forgotten, mid-1980s Kent bowling figures in Benson and Hedges Cup zonal matches – was amazed when I first heard Americans talk about baseball. They knew everything. Batting averages, salaries, games won, 'runs batted in', the on-base slugging average. The media saw to it that no significant number was left on its own: if it could be tabulated or turned into a graph, you could be certain that if the *New York Times* didn't run it the *Daily News* would.

No one – on the pitching mound, in the field or at-bat – escapes judgement by numbers. If you want to know how a batter performs under pressure, when he has two strikes against him, the relevant numbers will be in every broadsheet. And is he any good against left-handers? How does he fare in the big games in the post-season, when it's do-or-die stuff?

What's that pitcher like when he has 'fallen behind the batter' (thrown more balls than strikes)? And that centre-fielder – he's fast and athletic, but he only has a .817 fielding percentage. 'These days,' as Mark McGwire (he should know: he holds the record for the most number of home runs in a season) put it, 'they have a stat for how many times a guy goes for a cup of coffee.'

When I read the celebrated *New Yorker* columnist Roger Angell describing the baseball box-scoring system as 'one of my favourite urban flowers: a precisely etched miniature of the sport itself', I knew I had encountered a sport that took numbers seriously. Baseball's historical landmarks, in fact, are so deeply etched into the national consciousness that to many Americans, not just baseball fans, years have become synonymous with great baseball moments.

The year 1947 means Jackie Robinson, who became the first black man to play in modern major league baseball that season; 1961 means Roger Maris, who beat Babe Ruth's sixty home runs in a season; 1969 means the 'Miracle Mets', who won the pennant after a disastrous 1968 season (man walks on the moon, it must be admitted, also figures in typical memories of 1969); 1998 will perhaps be remembered as the year Mark McGwire passed Maris.

Baseball is a numbers game through and through. Four balls, three strikes, nine innings, 90 feet, a twenty-wins pitching season, a .300 hitter. Players know each other's statistics; fans know the players' statistics; the Hall of Fame preserves the best statistics for posterity. Numbers are baseball's crystalline essence.

In Game 2 of the Subway Series in 1998, Mike Hampton's poor pitching performance for the Mets demonstrated a classic example of baseball statistical super-analysis.

Hampton had been the Mets' MVP (Most Valuable Player) in the Mets' World Series eliminator the week before – what we would call the semi-final, but what Americans call the National League championship. But despite his great form running up to Game 2 at Yankee Stadium, it was clear after just a few pitches that something was wrong. Hampton's fast ball was 5 m.p.h. slower than normal, and his change-up wasn't pinpoint accurate. He is known as a tough competitor who loves the big stage, so it couldn't be big match nerves, could it?

The television commentators didn't think so. They blamed the weather. He didn't like the cold. Brought up in California and based in Houston, Texas, Hampton, the Fox statisticians quickly informed viewers, had lost 70 per cent of his games when it was colder than 55 degrees. It was 52 degrees and getting colder in Yankee Stadium that night.

The pundits were proved right: Hampton pitched unusually poorly all night. Perhaps Bobby Valentine should have looked at the long-range weather forecast; if he had, he might have played Hampton in Game 1, when it was a comfortable 60 degrees, and Al Leiter, a native New Yorker, in the chilly conditions of Game 2. Such is the attention to detail in baseball selection that, if the newspapers had announced

'Hampton swopped for Leiter: too cold for Mike', I doubt anyone would have batted an eyelid.

I couldn't help thinking about what would happen if that kind of statistic crept into county cricket. Overseas stars could suddenly find themselves left out of the team on crisp April mornings. Suppose the Kent statistician, for example, announced that Rahul Dravid – Kent's Indian overseas professional in 2000 – had a poor career record when the temperature was below 52 degrees. Would we have saved him for sunnier Canterbury days when he could close his eyes and think of Bangalore? (In reality, by the way, Rahul produced some of his best innings on particularly cold spring and autumn days.)

And how would in-form cricketers take to being dropped just because in previous years they had fared poorly against an upcoming opponent? It's a commonplace in baseball. Jose Vizcaino, the Yankee who struck the game-winning hit of Game 1, owed his presence on the field in Yankee Stadium to just such a selection. The Viz was not a regular starter. Yankee manager Joe Torre admitted he had only included him because the Mets pitcher was announced as being Al Leiter. While leafing through the man-on-man averages from previous Mets–Yankees games, Torre subsequently explained, 'Vizcaino's figures against Leiter just kinda jumped out at me.'

Hmm. 'Sorry, Ed', I imagined a cricket coach saying to me, 'I know you got a hundred last game, but the guy in the second team has a great record against their opening bowler so we're picking him for the Lord's final.' How would I take that? Not well, I suspect.

'I'd love to be a coach of an American sport,' one

professional cricket coach once told me. 'They don't mess around.' He is right. In baseball almost no statistic is inconceivable, nor any selection made without full reference to all the available evidence. The availability of critical evidence has a flip side for coaches: they haven't got much chance of bluffing their players or the media. Bullshitters don't last long.

The players, meanwhile, must get used to being constantly analysed and compared. And the bigger the fixture, the more intense the statistical microscope. Playing hard ball, they say in baseball, is a hard school.

Of course, the players get the bonuses too – massive salaries, endorsements, sponsorship, perks, fame, adulation – so we shouldn't get too dewy eyed about the enormous pressure of public expectation and, when things don't go right on the night, the inevitable finger-pointing that comes their way. After all, the British tabloid press can more than hold its own when it comes to heaping damnation upon the perceived perpetrators of national sporting disasters.

As for me, the next time I'm having a bad spell and I have to endure a depressing set of averages being pinned on the dressing-room wall, I'll remember that it's nothing compared to life in the baseball big leagues. In America, I doubt the players ever need to read any of the numerous statistics: they are reminded of them daily in every newspaper, on every radio show, and in the expressions on the faces of strangers they pass in the street.

That American phenomenon extends far beyond sport. The cult of relentless analysis informs every aspect of American public life, from baseball coverage to political journalism. In trying to take 'subjective' judgement out of the equation, and stick to hard evidence, the American media is not afraid of reshuffling the same information in countless different formats. So long as it's hard news, it's good news.

I had another glimpse of it four days before the presidential election in 2000, when a revelation about George W. Bush hit the front pages. Back on Labor Day in 1976, Bush had been pulled over by the police for driving too slowly a mile away from his parents' summer home in Kennebunkport, Maine. He was drunk. He had been made to pay a fine, and subsequently lost his licence.

Only now, twenty-four years on, had the story been leaked to the press. In an election that was 'too close to call', the press filled endless pages with detailed analysis about the Maine go-slow. It may be understandable that the media should be so interested in the past of a potential American President, but the level of scrutiny the story received (albeit for a short time) was almost unbelievable. Did Bush spend the night in jail? No. Was there an accident? No. How many beers did he have? Several. 'Several' would be more than two?

In Britain, the *Spectator*'s Mark Steyn saw the funny side: 'Another three minutes and they'd have been asking: Draught or bottled? Budweiser or Sam Adams? Or some filthy Canadian swill like Molson?' 'Never underestimate,' Steyn concluded, 'the capacity of the American media to bore any story into the ground.'

But I hadn't seen anything yet. When I went to an 'election party' – where we were supposed to stay until it was known in the early hours who the new President would be, which in this case would have meant a four-week sleep-over – I got to experience a real statistical jamboree. Peter Snow's beloved 'Swingometer', the one that has graced so many *Newsnight* specials after British general elections, was kids' stuff in comparison to what I was watching. There were so many multicoloured maps, swings, pie charts, predictions, and pundits – the people I watched it with insisted, of course, on flicking between all the channels to see which network was ahead of the game – that sometimes it was difficult to be sure whether the results we were seeing were projections or cast-iron 'closed deals'.

It was a distinction, I was reassured to discover, that was beyond everyone, including the vice-president. First Gore 'won' Florida and Republicans wept; then Bush 'won' it and Gore telephoned his rival to concede (which he later retracted); then Florida reverted to 'too close to call' – where it remained, as everyone now knows, for weeks thereafter. There was even a statistic on how statistically accurate electoral statistics were. Even if baseball statistics were bewildering, at least I knew who was winning.

Better still, one network installed a basketball-style shot-clock countdown watch on the bottom left-hand corner of the TV screen. Because of the numerous time zones of American states, local polling stations would close at various different times. The closing of a polling station, of course, had nothing whatsoever to do with the counting of votes or understanding the result of the election – but it was a definite event, hard news. 'And it's twenty, no eight . . . I mean fifteen seconds to poll closing time in Idaho, folks . . .' And then . . . nothing. Yep, the poll has closed and now we're *no further forward*. So let's get back to the blue, red and yellow pie chart and bring in a new psephologist.

If I had seen all that before I watched the World Series, I wouldn't have been surprised by discussion of Mike Piazza's hitting average against Roger Clemens, or Mike Hampton's record in the cold, or Todd Zeile's average against left-handed curve balls. It's typical of the American media's tireless (but sometimes exhausting) attention to detail. There's a number for everything, which is occasionally revealing, often beguiling, and frequently amusing.

At times, I admired the rigour of American reporting and analysis. On other occasions, it seemed to be an excuse among journalists for not having any ideas of their own. I have listened to countless American journalists lambast the British media for being sloppy and impressionistic. Conversely, we Brits sometimes find earnestly fact-checked, pseudo-scientific American reporting – whether it concerns a presidential election or the World Series – plain ridiculous.

Perhaps the cult of objective analysis is part of the greater American obsession with expertise. Someone once said that everyone in New York thinks he is 'either a genius or a connoisseur'. The self-styled connoisseurs are certainly plentiful. And it isn't unknown for a young Brit – if he were so brave as to venture an opinion on a subject beyond his immediate sphere of expertise – to be perceived as 'opinionated'. Sometimes the Land of the Free is not so free from hierarchy and deference as it supposes.

12
BOOKS AND SPORTS

It is often said that cricket has a great literature. Compared to other English team sports, it does – but that isn't saying much. The best English writers, until very recently, have largely ignored sport, particularly team sport, as literary material. We have been well served by sports reporting, but less so by historical sports books and sporting novels.

That has not been the case in America, where there has never been such an iron curtain between literature and sport. Not that I knew anything about American sports writing until I went there. When a friend of mine put me in touch with the sportswriter George Plimpton so that I could grill him with baseball questions, he lent me a small library of his favourite American sports books. Among them were *Bang the Drum, Slowly*, a baseball novel by Mark Harris; Roger Kahn's *The Boys of Summer*; *You Know Me Al*, by Ring Lardner; and *The Norton Book of Sports*, which Plimpton had edited himself.

I was about to start reading books that were more

intelligent, more moving, more involved, simply better than I had previously imagined any sports books could be. I had been formally introduced to the world of American sports writing – and I would come to love it. The British might not like to admit that America can teach us cultural lessons, but in the case of sports books we have no choice. From Ernest Hemingway's glorification of bull-fighting to John Updike's examination of the mores of golf, major American writers have been infinitely more prepared than their British counterparts to write about sport.

Take George Will – thinking conservative's conservative, Pulitzer Prize-winner and syndicated columnist whose articles appear weekly in 480 newspapers. Will once quipped that he hoped one day to graduate from the political pages to the sports desk. He hasn't quite finished with politics yet, but he has written a number one bestseller about professional baseball, *Men at Work: The Craft of Baseball*. Will exhaustively interviewed a pitcher, a batter, an infielder and a manager in an attempt to understand their quest for technical and psychological perfection. In terms of pure intellectual rigour, it must rank as one of the best sports books ever written. Imagine Matthew Parris, now that he has retired from his *Times* parliamentary sketch, focusing his entire critical intelligence on the subject of cricket (not an easy conceit, I admit) and you have *Men at Work*.

George Will is one of many American intellectual sports writers. David Remnick, winner of the Pulitzer Prize for *Lenin's Tomb*, a book about the fracturing of the Soviet Union, and editor of *The New Yorker*, recently published *King of the World*, an award-winning biography of Muhammad Ali. David

Halberstam, the former *New York Times* reporter whose trenchant reports from Saigon helped to turn the American establishment against the Vietnam War, may be remembered as much for his book about the golden baseball season of 1947 and his brilliant study of rowing, *The Amateurs*. Richard Ben Kramer, who also won the Pulitzer Prize for his dispatches from the Middle East, abandoned international affairs to turn his attentions to the story of Yankee legend Joe DiMaggio. Plimpton's own career, which has ranged freely from editing the highbrow, intellectual magazine *The Paris Review* to pitching as an amateur in the All-Star game, has demonstrated how well the cross-over between sport and literature can work.

It is hard to come up with British equivalents. Neville Cardus was a writer of purple prose, but he was generally more interested in the mythology of cricket than the game itself. And we have some warm-hearted novels and memoirs about the amateur sporting idyll, such as Hugh de Selincourt's *The Cricket Match*. And more recently Roger Scruton, disturbed by New Labour's attack on old Britain as much as the narrower issue of hunting itself, came up with *On Fox Hunting*. England can also boast the late Alan Ross, editor of *London Magazine*, poet and fine cricket writer – though, personally, I was never convinced of his grasp of the modern game. There are others – of course there are – but not as many as there might be.

The business of professional sport in Britain has generally been particularly poorly served. The shelves in WHSmith strain under the weight of piles of ghosted memoirs – some of which, like those by Tony Adams and Tony Cascarino, are very good. But exposés aside, it is much harder to find a real tradition of sports literature on this side of the Atlantic.

Post-*Fever Pitch*, British sports writing is definitely perking up. But there is no indication yet that Charles Moore, editor of the *Daily Telegraph*, is researching a book about professional football, or that Simon Jenkins is planning a treatise on cricket, or that Simon Schama's next volume will be called *Landscape and Tennis*.

Britain has plenty of excellent sports journalists (I would particularly like this message to get through to all the journalists who are down to watch Kent this year: how I admire you all), my favourite, as you will have spotted, being Simon Barnes. But during his early days as a cub sports reporter, even Barnes was hauled aside by his boss: 'Don't get no fancy ideas, son, or silly high-flown notions of literary worth.' If that's your aim, you'd better stick to opera or politics.

What no one has ever explained, so far as I am aware, is *why* the British have been so reluctant to write seriously about sport. One explanation, I think, can be found in the influence of the Victorian idea that sport is primarily a means to becoming a better person rather than an end in itself.

National myths change so quickly and cover their tracks so efficiently that it is easy to forget how new some of them are. We might imagine that organised sport has been a part of national life since the year dot, but it was only in the 1860s that the British heavily invested in organised sports as a means of educating the young. Instead of sketching plants in botanical gardens, as previous generations of pupils had been encouraged to do, the new generation of public schoolboys was sent out on to the games field when the day's lessons ended. In the world picture of Muscular Christianity – championed by Thomas Arnold, Charles Kingsley and Edward Thring – sport was a catch-all cure for the vices of youth. (It had to be properly played, of course – fairly and never for profit.)

With a growing demand for reliable civil servants and soldiers to man her increasingly global Empire, Britain needed to promote the values of leadership and fair play. No wonder the taking part was more important than the winning: what use would it have been if the poor ex-public school souls holed up in Calcutta doing the Empire's tax returns had been trained to score individualist tries as adolescent rugby players? As adults, in the game of real life, they might have run off with the booty. Those school mottos which echoed around every English school rugby pitch and cricket square from 1860 to 1950 – honour, duty, sacrifice, responsibility – had a definite purpose. They had to produce gentlemen, a caste to which you could increasingly belong if you *behaved* like a gentleman even if you had been born into anything but gentility.

But by promoting the educative and moralising powers of sport, the amateur ideal – for all its virtues – inevitably downgraded the process of trying to win, the search for perfection, the acquisition of glory and the despair of failure. These are far better literary subjects than fair play and 'playing the game' and all those other pieties which dominate the sporting literature of late nineteenth-century and early twentieth-century England. *Roy of the Rovers*-style heroism may be amusing to reread as social history, but it is rarely enduring art. Authors who determinedly occupy only the moral high ground tend to produce only lowbrow literature.

While the legacy of Empire lived on in Britain, sport remained too sacred to inspire realistic literature. The idyll of amateur sport, the *communion* of village cricket – the vista, the parson, the tea – was fine as a novelistic social backdrop. But the muddied knees and dressing-room arguments and wage disputes of professional sport – the real drama, in other words – were completely out of the question. Only in the late twentieth century – as the onset of professionalism dragged British sports into the modern age, and forced people to accept that sport is a means in itself not just a way of becoming a better person – have we produced good books about sport the reality, not sport the abstraction.

The turning point was Nick Hornby's *Fever Pitch*. The media bandwagon success it inspired was scarcely believable: even chippy sport cynics could be seen with copies of *Fever Pitch* tucked under their arms on the London Tube. Could it be true? London's liberal media establishment was reading the autobiography of a bleakly obsessive Arsenal fan who was terrified of dying in the off season – and hence never knowing who won the Championship that year. Football, usually seen as the lowest of lowbrow sports, was suddenly serious stuff.

A few years later, when I was living in London just off the Fulham Road, I used to watch West London's Euro-trendies walk past my house on the way to watch Chelsea at Stamford Bridge. They were squeezing in a little football, one imagined, between sipping a latte or two at the Blue Bird Café on the King's Road and picking at a little Pasta alla Vialli in San Lorenzo's in Beauchamp Place.

More revolutionary still was the decision by the resolutely highbrow *Spectator* to print a weekly sports column. The publishers Random House, too, have tried to promote post-Hornby sports writing by establishing its Yellow Jersey imprint, which has already published A. L. Kennedy's *On Bullfighting*.

London has for some years boasted a wonderful sports bookshop – Sportspages on Charing Cross Road. But most of the books on its shelves seem to be American. True, soccer books are their bestseller. But the Sportspages manager told me that he suspected the popularity of football books owed more to the game's huge fan base than the literary merit of the books. And which sport came second? Baseball. 'Even though not many people play baseball in England,' he said, 'the books are so good that they sell themselves.'

The high quality of American sports writing is not a new phenomenon. It stretches back to the beginning of the twentieth century, long before most Englishmen thought professional sport was a worthy career, let alone sufficiently profound to inspire great literature. Perhaps it is no coincidence that the Victorian amateur sporting ideal was not promoted among Americans as much as by the Empire-orientated British.

The rhetoric of the amateur sporting ideal and gentility was not absent in America, but it was muted. As the American Heywood Broun put it in 1900, 'The tradition of professional baseball has always been agreeably free of chivalry. The rule is: do anything you can get away with.' Now *that's* good literary material . . .

To the ancient Greeks, significantly, sport was about winning, not taking part. 'Playing the game' is one of those ideas for which it is difficult to find a Greek translation. Playing good sport was more important than being 'a good sport'. The poems and songs dedicated to the victors attest to the fact that the literary minds of the day agreed. I don't want to overplay the causal link – it is only a hunch, not a fact – but it seems no coincidence that sporting literature has flourished where sport has not been too excessively moralised and gentrified. When confronted with the pieties of improbable sporting selflessness and empathy for the loser, writers have tended to look the other way.

American sports, of course, embraced professionalism and commercialism much earlier than their English equivalents. One writer referred to Sportsman's Park, home of the St Louis Browns, as a 'saloon with a baseball attachment'. The legendary sports manufacturer and baseball magnate A. G. Spalding even defended the right of fans to attack umpires: he said it was their democratic right as Americans to oppose tyranny in any form. Exploitative owners, players' strikes, crowd violence and match fixing were not modern baseball developments: they had been there from the start.

George Bernard Shaw, with a typically writerly nose for discord, much preferred the rough and tumble of the baseball diamond to the ironed whites of the cricket square. 'What is surprising and delightful,' he wrote, 'is that the spectators are allowed, and even expected, to join in the vocal part of the game. I do not see why this should not be introduced into cricket. There is no reason why the field should not try to put the batsman off his stroke at the critical moment by neatly timed disparagements of his wife's fidelity and his mother's respectability.' Shaw, it appears, would have enjoyed modern cricket more than the good old days of 'walking' and cap doffing.

Baseball, according to Ty Cobb, was 'something like a war'. A legendary 'spiker' of opponents, he used to sharpen his spikes before his turn at the bat, shouting to the first base-man, 'I'm coming to get you.' That was in the 1910s. John McGraw, 'toughest of the toughs', liked to spike umpires rather than opponents. 'I've seen umpires bathe their feet by the hour,' one sportswriter remembered, 'after McGraw spiked them through their shoes.'

It was a tough professional world, where innocent farm boys were exploited until they had thrown their last pitch. You got wise or you got used. That was the world which Ring Lardner brilliantly captured in his 1916 novel *You Know Me Al*, and Mark Harris echoed in 1946 with *Bang the Drum, Slowly* – respectively eighty and fifty years before Nick Hornby broke the British literary taboo about professional sport. Baseball knew no genteel idyll, nor even a façade of amateur civility. But it did get the books.

For a while I subconsciously accepted those outdated English conventions about sports literature. I always wanted to be a cricketer and a writer; but I never wanted to be a cricketer and a *sports*writer. It is perverse, really, given that cricket is what I love and know most about. Even in the depths of winter, when I don't have a game for months, it occupies an irrational amount of my time. I often think about what I've done wrong in the past, trying to remember my thought processes when I had success, and think about ways I can get better. Cricket, particularly batting, is my primary obsession.

And yet I never thought I would write about sport, least of all my own game. Cricket was off limits – and as a result my best material never made it on to the word processor.

In fact, I'd write about anything else. I've written *Sunday Telegraph* book reviews about novels with plots so distant from my own experience that they are scarcely part of the world I inhabit. At university, I even thought about trying to write a book about Wagner, who I was studying at the time, despite the fact that I am neither a musicologist nor a German-speaker. I have started several op-ed pieces, most of which turned out to be unsubmitted false starts, about 'issues of the day' – despite the fact that I rarely had any original insights, just a slight spin on other people's ideas.

What I did know about was playing cricket six months a year. But what use was that to a writer? Playing professional sport was fine; but writing about it? People used to advise me, 'keep your life as a writer separate from your life as a sports-man'. Yes, of course, I used to say.

That's all complete nonsense. Sport is as worthy of serious analysis as any other sphere of human activity. Much better advice would have been 'write about what you know'.

But why write at all? Why not concentrate on cricket? You've got the rest of your life to write. People often say that to me, as though I am critically neglecting my cricket every time I switch on my computer. 'How can you expect to make runs when you are always reading?' W. G. Grace once said to a struggling Gloucestershire colleague, 'You don't ever catch me that way.' If he was that critical of a sportsman reading, what would he have thought of one *writing*?

In my case, I think writing about cricket helps me not to

'obsess' too much, as Americans say. It gets things out of my system. Talking about a challenging experience, as everyone knows, often helps to make it seem more manageable. For a writer, the problem there is that talking things through sometimes feels like a waste of good material. Why not put it down on paper? In that sense, when I did turn to writing about sport, it helped to clarify my mind about things I had experienced. The process of writing was like an exorcism and conversation with a confidant all in one.

I was interested to read Steve Waugh make a similar point in the December 2000 edition of *Wisden* magazine. He said that the mental discipline of writing his diary for one or two hours every night – even during Test matches – had helped his batting. It was fun, he said; it provided him with a complementary challenge; and the discipline he learnt from writing helped his on-field discipline.

If it's good enough for Steve Waugh . . .

13

A NATIONAL
SPORTING TEMPERAMENT?

Steve Waugh? W. G. Grace? Who are they anyway? When talking cricket with Americans, I had to get used to such questions. In more optimistic moments while I was writing this book, I had hoped that New Yorkers might move towards cricket in the same way that I was moving towards baseball. An unlikely, romantic notion, I admit, but at some illogical level I thought that the more I enthused about baseball, the more interest they might take in my game.

I haven't been exactly overburdened with American cricket converts asking me to explain the nuances of the game to them. Generally, if I stay on their territory, everything is hunky-dory. But if the conversation moves too far into the unknown – stumps, spinners or square cuts – it tends to lose energy. I've certainly had some interesting responses over the years. 'Cricket? That's the game where you hit coloured balls through hoops in the ground, right?' asked one of them.

On luckier days I'd get a nod of comprehension, followed by, 'Oh, you're a cricket*eer*' – as if stressing the last syllable, as in 'musketeer', helped them to grasp the true nature of the animal before them. Eventually I stopped correcting the error and went straight in with cricket*eer*. Even then, they would sometimes need convincing that it was a real job. 'Now tell me, Edward, can you . . . I mean . . . you know, like, make a *living* from doing this cricket*eer*ing stuff?'

Once, when I was moving into a new apartment, I carried my cricket bat on to the subway. Until then I had thought it was almost impossible to draw attention to oneself on the Lexington Avenue Express: multipierced midriffs, green hair, almost total nakedness, public displays of almost any sexual persuasion you can imagine (and a few you can't) – they've seen it all before and don't bat an eyelid. But my Slazenger V500 cricket bat was clearly a sufficiently genuine novelty to become the focus of several bemused expressions. 'What have we got *here*', they seemed to be thinking.

I have had some nice comments, too. When I went to one New York Hallowe'en party dressed as a cricketer, several Indian taxi drivers pulled up in the street, saying 'Go hit a six, man!', or 'It's about time I saw a cricketer in New York!'

At the party I felt seriously eccentric. In a city where black is the universal uniform, wearing all white means you're either a loony or an anachronism. 'Are you a polo player?' No. 'A tennis player?' No. 'That British accent you do is really realistic.'

I could have been forgiven for thinking that cricket was as alien to American culture as Morris dancing or Guy Fawkes Night. Perhaps I shouldn't have been surprised. I've heard countless English cricket fans say 'cricket just wouldn't suit America, would it?'. Too slow, too languid, insufficiently macho. As Henry Chadwick, the Englishman who helped to organise and define American baseball in its early days, put it in 1850: 'Americans do not care to dawdle – what they do, they want to do in a hurry. In baseball, all is lightning. Thus the reason for American antipathy to cricket can be readily understood.'

The truth is very different. For much of the nineteenth century cricket was America's favourite team game. In 1850 cricket clubs flourished in 125 American towns and cities across twenty-two states. America also took part in the first ever cricket international, which was not, as you might expect, a battle between England and Australia, but the 1844 'Test' between Canada and the United States. And in 1858, when the landscape architects of New York's new Central Park had to name the area allocated for ball games, they came up with 'the Cricket Ground' – much to the despair of base-ball's early supporters.

It was in fact not the rules of cricket that didn't suit America; it was its Englishness. As the *New York Times* put it in 1857, 'to reproduce the tastes and habits of the English sporting life in this country is neither possible nor desirable'. English sports like cricket, despite the fact that many Americans enjoyed them, were labelled as unpatriotic.

Baseball came along at just the right time to tap into those anti-English sentiments. Though it, too, was derived from the English sports of cricket and rounders, there was enough mystery about baseball's origins to drape Old Glory all over America's new game. It suited America's 'yearning for a game', as the sports newspaper *Porter's Spirit of the Times* put it, 'peculiar to the citizens of the United States, one distinctive from the games of the British, like cricket'.

America was ready for a sport that expressed its burgeoning self-confidence. Baseball was the ticket. Though its first official set of rules was only codified in 1846, within a decade Walt Whitman would announce: 'Well – it's *our* game. That's the chief fact in connection to it; it has the snap, go fling of the American atmosphere; it belongs as much to our institutions, fits into them as significantly as our Constitution's laws; is just as important in the sum total of our historic life.' Swift work for a new game.

From the outset, baseball would be perceived by Americans as 'our game' – not partly American, or largely American, but independently and exclusively American, perhaps more so than any sport has ever belonged to one country's self-invention. Play baseball and be a real American: that was the message.

There was one nagging problem: baseball's derivation from cricket and rounders, which fatally linked it with Englishness. It had to be got rid of. The 1888 'All-Star' World Tour – Australia, Egypt and Italy were among the overseas destinations – led by sporting goods manufacturer Albert G. Spalding, provided a perfect opportunity. On their return to America, despite having failed to spread baseball fever as successfully as they had hoped, baseball's first evangelists were welcomed home with a vast celebration banquet. The President of the National League repeatedly announced during his speech that baseball's origins were distinctly American, and completely unconnected with any inferior English ball games. The guests began to chant, 'No rounders! No rounders! No rounders!'

But it was not enough: rumours of baseball's English

inheritance persisted. Spalding became so chafed that he eventually persuaded a friendly senator to authorise him and some carefully chosen friends to form an investigative commission to determine the origins of the game. In 1908, the commission solemnly gave its verdict: the game had been invented by Abner Doubleday in 1839 in Cooperstown, in upstate New York. Doubleday based his sport, the commission maintained, on a traditional American children's game called 'one old cat'. Not a cricket ball in sight.

It's a nice story. A pity, then, that Doubleday spent that summer of 1839 as an army officer cadet at West Point, nowhere near Cooperstown, preparing for a military career that would see him rise to the rank of general and fight in the Civil War, and earn him a handsome *New York Times* obituary, and one which did not even mention baseball. Baseball's myth of immaculate conception had been formulated on the basis of a letter from an elderly man who later died in an asylum for the insane. But the game had been furnished with just the kind of founding father it needed: a hero, a soldier, an American.

Spalding was now able to proclaim that baseball really was the national game: played by Americans, watched by Americans, invented by Americans. It struck a chord, and the myth of baseball's American-ness was well received. By 1908, the sports writer Tim Munrane was arguing that 'there are two things I teach the boys that are all-American – one's the good old flag and one's baseball'.

If you repeat something often enough, people start to believe it. That is the art of propaganda. And so it has been with the diverging reputations of cricket and baseball in

America. One sank into relative obscurity, receding into wealthy pockets of Anglophilia along the east coast. The other became a form of national sporting communion. But neither trend was predestined by an American temperamental aversion to cricket.

If cricket stalled in America because of its Englishness, did baseball fail to take root in England because of its American overtones? Though Jane Austen mentioned a game of 'baseball' in her 1798 novel *Northanger Abbey*, organised baseball didn't arrive in England until the 1890s. Four teams, Derby County, Preston North End, Aston Villa and Stoke City – all with close ties to association football clubs – formed their own baseball league. But the experiment didn't last long and the league collapsed in 1911.

Perhaps the timing of baseball's first British excursion was unfortunate. In the late nineteenth century, English cricket underwent a philosophical shift of emphasis. The game's administration was removed from the hands of mercenary professionals like William Clarke and Fred Lillywhite and came under the control of the more gentlemanly and socially exclusive MCC. Cricket was re-inventing itself as a self-improving pastime.

Cricket's shots soon became part of a moral index. 'The straight bat' aimed towards the off was not only the epitome of style but also the hallmark of moral rectitude. Good boys played straight. The young B. J. T. Bosanquet, the inventor of the googly, was threatened with expulsion from Eton if he attempted any more uneducated shots.

Shots like the hook or the pull – or any stroke that required a baseball-style across-the-body-swing – were simply 'not cricket'. According to W. G. Grace, 'Young batsmen should be severely reprimanded if they show any tendency towards pulling!' Lucky I didn't play in the 1890s, then.

If the moralising attitude of the 'straight bat' cannot have helped baseball take root in England, nor can the early twentieth-century clamp down against 'throwers', which ruined a number of famous cricket careers and forced C. B. Fry to give up bowling altogether. It is an imprecise historical deduction, but it might be that cricket's turn-of-the-century obsession with the straight bat and the straight arm made baseball seem too vulgar to the newly defined English tastes.

Baseball made another appearance in England in the 1930s, this time in the north of England, where Yorkshire League baseball crowds regularly attracted 5,000 spectators. But even the arrival of a million and a half American servicemen during the Second World War couldn't push baseball into the mainstream. Their exhibition games at Wembley drew large crowds at the time, but as the memory of war receded so too did the British affection for baseball.

Baseball's prospects in England, in fact, are better today than they have ever been. As part of a huge worldwide outreach programme, Major League Baseball claims to have introduced 200,000 young Britons to baseball in the last year. MLB certainly has the money and the organisation to spread the baseball word far and wide. And cricket, already squeezed by the football season's encroachment into late summer, may soon have a serious new summer rival.

But it needn't necessarily be an either/or choice. In Australia, where baseball is played far more seriously than in England, both games have fruitfully co-existed. Several

Australians have made it into the American major leagues, and a handful of their best Test cricketers over the years – Neil Harvey, Norm O'Neill, Bill Lawry, Ian and Greg Chappell among them – also played amateur baseball.

So much for baseball in cricketing countries. Can cricket come back Stateside? It has shown some signs of recovery. India and Pakistan now play one-dayers in Canada and California, and a new wave of Asian immigrants to Silicon Valley has inspired dozens of new cricket leagues. And in the old cricket stronghold of the north east, Jamaican immigrants have set up new cricket pitches all over the outer boroughs of New York. Stranger things have happened than an American cricketing renaissance. Or perhaps, having seen how money follows American taste, I am just dreaming of a vast influx of American cash.

Renaissance or not, cricket has at least managed to secure a foothold in one of the unlikeliest of all locations, the ghettos of African-American Los Angeles. When I found out cricket had reached Compton and South Central, I decided I had to go and see how well gangsters played the cover drive.

Cricket in Compton is the master plan of social activist Ted Hayes, a black forty-year-old who lived voluntarily on the streets for twelve years so as to understand better the plight of LA's poor. Then he found cricket. He now believes that the civilising influence of cricket can turn the street fighters of gang-infested Compton and South Central into gentlemen. One weekend in December, I went to see them.

Compton, the inspiration for John Singleton's dystopian film *Boyz in the Hood*, boasts a murder rate twice that of San Francisco, a city seven times its size. It is perhaps the most infamous suburb in any American city, not only because of its frequent gangland drive-by shootings, but because of its penchant for glamourising them. Gangsta rap, with its laid back beats and graphically violent lyrics, was born in Compton and South Central. It can list Snoop Doggy Dogg, Coolio and Warren G among its alumni.

Manhattan, Tom Wolfe once said, is not really America but an offshore shopping boutique. Now I was about to see the other side of American urban life.

Before seeing the prize draw of cricket in Compton, I was due to meet Ted Hayes at an elaborate British film function at the Beverly Hills Hotel where he was hoping to win over new converts to his grand scheme. So when I turned up at the LAX Avis car hire bureau at the airport, I was wearing my best suit for the Beverly Hills lunch, not thinking that it might make me look even more ridiculous when I arrived in the ghetto. 'You're driving to Compton, in *that*,' the car rental assistant said, pointing at my Armani suit. 'Good luck, kiddo!'

What if I broke down, I suddenly thought. What if I got lost? What if I stopped too long at a traffic light?

But it was a sunny morning in Los Angeles, and my red metallic car was gleaming in a most pleasing Californian way. I'd be fine. I had looked briefly at a map at Avis, and it was an easy trip to Beverly Hills – no need to plan a route too precisely, it was just up a bit and left a bit. No problem. Within five minutes of driving out of the airport I had the window down and the radio up. Sunset Boulevard here we come.

Things quickly went wrong. First I took the freeway going east rather than west, before quickly losing track of the signs altogether. If you're new to LA, it's a confusing place. One

suburb seamlessly rolls into another, and, at first, it's difficult
to tell the rich areas from the poor. It's nothing like crossing
from Manhattan into the Bronx, where the derelict ware-
houses and burnt-out apartment blocks quickly confirm that
you've changed scene. Even the worst suburbs of LA have
rows of detached houses with small front yards and parked
cars. In other words, if you're an outsider, you don't know
when you're entering a war zone.

After an hour of confusion, I ended up forty miles away
from Beverly Hills and hurtling ever deeper into the
unknown. Panic set in. Isn't this what happened at the start of
Bonfire of the Vanities? Yes, that's right – wrong turn, wrong
suburb, unfortunate accident, white man in suit, hostile surroundings, spiralling disaster . . . Christ, lost in the murder
capital of America! Right that's it! Radio off, pull over, ask
someone!

I took the next turning off the highway. I asked for directions in two shops, then a gas station, only to elicit confused
replies – in Chinese. Everyone on the street was Chinese.
Perhaps I was in Chinatown? I'd seen the Jack Nicholson
movie. The area's reputation looms like a heavy shadow over
the whole film – it is always avoided and only discussed in
hushed tones. Even Big Jack was wary of Chinatown. No
wonder I was terrified. *Chinatown* and *Bonfire of the Vanities*
rolled into one increasingly vivid nightmare. Get back in the
car.

Sitting by the highway with the car doors locked, I rifled
through the bumph Avis had given me and found a small
road map. Keep driving till you find a road going west until
you hit the Pacific Ocean. Then, even if you're nowhere near

where you are trying to get to, you'll have some idea where you are. And concentrate this time.

I hit the ocean at Santa Monica. I'd heard of Santa Monica and they even spoke English there. I soon managed to get detailed instructions to the Beverly Hills Hotel. Panic over, I made the rest of the short trip up Wilshire Boulevard relatively easily. I have never been so glad to see a room full of two thousand complete strangers. Compton would be easy, surely, after that journey?

After lunch in the vast and soulless dining room – complete with true Tinsletown chandeliers – Ted took me to his homeless shelter. The Dome Village, which nestles under a freeway in the shadow of downtown LA, consists of twelve igloo-shaped huts, each sleeping two or three homeless teenagers. It was a bad day for Ted; one of the huts had burnt down in the night, and, though no one was hurt, three people's belongings had been ruined. I went in to the hut, really nothing more than an insulated tent, to survey the damage. In the smouldering rubble, I could see a charred Gray Nicolls Scoop cricket bat, just like one I had used as a ten-year-old, and a pair of blackened buckle-strap pads. It was a dramatically unexpected image. It was also my first experience of classic journalistic mixed emotions: their tragedy was my story.

It was a warm and cloudless December morning, so Ted demanded a cricket practice at a local Compton school. Seven of the team got into Ted's white van, and I took the other four in my hire car. One of them, the wicket-keeper, had once belonged to a gang called the Killer Society. His friend, he told me as we drove along the freeway, was in jail on a murder charge after a drive-by shooting. 'It's sad, man, he could have been a good opening batsman.'

'What happens in a drive-by?' I asked. Sniggers of incomprehension from the back seat. 'Simple. You just drive-by someone when they're outside their house and shoot 'em.' *I see.* This was worse than the Kent dressing room. 'But Ted's got us out of all that now. We play the game with a straight bat now.' If I had been fabricating conversations for the piece, I wouldn't have dared put it so well.

Ted himself turned out to be a dream interviewee – charming, talkative, and full of perfect soundbites. 'We gotta swop the gat [LA slang for gun],' he told me, 'for the bat.' He bemoaned the commercialism and brashness of contemporary American sports – 'baseballers these days are as bad as footballers' – and refused to let any contradictory evidence influence his view that cricket is still played in a spirit of perfect gentility and sportsmanship. It suited his mission. 'We've got to teach these kids not to argue with the umpire and to walk when they edge it to the 'keeper.'

Ted had heard on the Discovery Channel that the Victorians thought there was more to sport than winning; now it is the centrepiece of his social philosophy for LA. 'Those stripy-capped Edwardian cricketers,' a dreadlocked African-American was explaining to me, 'had it right, not that poncy braggart Muhammad Ali.' C. B. Fry: hero to LA's criminal youth? If I couldn't get a story out of all that, I thought to myself, I should give up the writing and stick to cricket.

'Just think of the irony,' Hayes told me as I left the Dome Village. 'A group of homeless people are bringing the noble English game of cricket to the notoriously gang-infested ghettos of LA. If we can do that, it shows that anything is possible.'

But the phenomenon of cricket in Compton is a charming eddy of counter-culture running against the flow of social and sporting evolution. To some extent being 'a gentleman' in England is not seen, perhaps with good reason, as 'the future'. For most aspiring English actors, developing a 'mockney' accent is a far shrewder move than assuming Hugh Grant-style foppery. Modern cricketers, too, must be 'pros' now in everything they do. Until the wheel turns again, gentility will only be for the gangsters.

A different version of my trip to see LA's gangster crick-eters, incidently, first appeared in the London-based *Prospect* magazine. An American magazine called the *Utne Reader* sub-sequently bought it for publication in America, which, because I hadn't heard of it, I mistakenly assumed nobody read. But when I was introduced as a professional cricketer to a journalist in New York the following autumn, he told me to read a piece in the July *Utne Reader* about cricket in Compton. It felt like listening to an audience applauding a speech you had written for someone else to deliver. Not all my articles, I thought, go unread before they become wrap-ping for fish and chips.

The new trend of gangster cricket has not yet, however, hit the mainstream of American culture. Typically, those Americans who have heard of cricket – and who don't confuse it with croquet or lacrosse – still assume it is anachronistic and class-ridden. They would agree with George Orwell, who wrote in 1944 that 'cricket is not a twentieth-century game, and nearly all modern-minded people dislike it'. 'Ah yes, cricket,' Americans say, 'monied white gentlemen out for a leisurely afternoon stroll!'

It is an ironic misconception. Far from being confined to one single social milieu, cricket is one of the great cross-class games, a point sadly missed by Americans. They should know better, given their predilection for a classless society.

When I wasn't dispelling the myth that cricket is all gin and tonics and jazz caps, I also used to enjoy pointing out to Americans that cricket is the second most popular team game in the world. Far from being a fading anachronism, it is also – thanks to the subcontinent – the fastest growing in terms of fan base. Cricket is not in decline; its power axis has shifted.

But despite my best efforts to portray cricket as sexy, global and forward-looking – 'You know there were thirty million, yes *million*, page hits on the county scores on CricInfo.com last season' – I usually felt I was banging my head against a brick wall. In Manhattan, I eventually had to accept that being a cricketer has only a certain cachet.

How things changed when I started writing a book about baseball. Suddenly, I felt as if I'd been handed the keys to the city. 'I never have trouble making conversation with people,' Frederick C. Klein said. 'All I have to do is tell them I write about sports and they open right up.' Baseball: now there was a game, people purred. Good for you . . . they said . . . even if you are a Brit.

In my new context, it was easy, later in the conversation, to slip in quietly that I was also a cricketer. Better still: he's come to find out how it's done properly, they thought. My taking an interest in their favourite summer sport was a perfect piece of cultural flattery.

Only once did my baseball connection cause a wrong turn in a social event. At a SoHo party attended mostly by European baseball atheists wearing black, an Italian graphic designer was recounting his reflections on Yankee Stadium. 'Once you've eaten the hot dog,' he began, 'and drunk a beer or two, and admired the view, the true horror of the evening hits you: the distractions are over and there's nothing else to do but watch the game . . . which is *so* boring. The guy who'd dragged me there kept on excitedly pointing out all the signals the manager was giving to the players. Even he didn't know what they actually meant, so how could he possibly expect me to be interested? I never thought I'd say this, but baseball's even worse than *cricket*.'

When another guest (who later admitted to me she'd agreed with him anyway) sensitively pointed out to him that I was, in fact, a cricketer who had come to America to write a book about baseball, he blurted out: 'God, what else is wrong with you?'

14

MORE THAN JUST GAMES

We now know that Abner Doubleday did not invent baseball in Cooperstown out of a traditional American children's game called 'one old cat'. No matter. Like all good quasi-religions, baseball needed a place for its pilgrims to visit and Cooperstown fitted the bill. Even now, anyone who delves into the history and culture of baseball cannot avoid repeatedly stumbling upon that small town in a downbeat corner of upstate New York, halfway between New York City and Lake Ontario.

Cooperstown boasts both the Hall of Fame and most of baseball's major museums. The Hall of Fame, in particular, is much more than just a tourist attraction. It crops up everywhere. 'You can't deliver a pitch like that to a future Hall of Famer like Barry Bonds,' TV commentators will often say, 'and expect not to get punished.' Ex-players turned pundits carry around the epithet 'Hall of Famer' like an extra limb. In cricket, we argue about who were the truly great players. In baseball, they vote on it – and the winners go to the Hall of Fame. It's that black and white. Or white and white – given that African-Americans weren't allowed into the Major Leagues until 1947.

I'd read a great deal about Cooperstown. Tom Boswell, the *Washington Post*'s respected baseball writer, described it as 'one extended family', in which 'everyone assumed everyone was friend'. To Boswell, Cooperstown is what all of America should be like, a world of historical resonance, shared values and perfect manners.

There was an assumption in the air that baseball – akin to religion – implied some sort of shared value system. In Cooperstown, you feel close to the game's nineteenth-century roots. The town is not much more than a hamlet, set amid small green mountains at the tip of a long, narrow strip of lake . . . It's a surprise to discover that the town's clocks actually move or that Coke costs more than a nickel. You expect everyone to be a farmer, tavernkeeper or blacksmith. In Cooperstown, you find yourself wondering, what does baseball believe in or stand for? That weekend I decided that baseball believes in reality and stands for moderation and insight in the face of that reality.

Keen to find out what baseball truly believes in and stands for, and whether the clocks do move, I set off one windy December morning, nickel in hand, on the five-hour drive from Manhattan to Cooperstown, up the Hudson valley, the Catskills to my left, west Connecticut and Massachusetts to my right, towards Canada, the lakes and into the teeth of an oncoming blizzard.

Upstate New York, for some reason, has mostly missed out on the patchy gentrification of rural New England. Vermont got the outlet boutiques, the cappuccinos and the fancy B&Bs; upstate New York generally got stuck with farming. With each hour on the road, as the snowflakes grew bigger and the towns smaller, it seemed more unlikely that I was indeed heading towards baseball's Mecca. How did they drag Babe Ruth this far from his suite at the glitzy Algonquin Hotel? In a way, it is appropriate: baseball, despite being the most urban of games, has always inspired waves of rural nostalgia. Perhaps only somewhere as off the beaten track as Cooperstown would do.

You can tell a lot about a place by its signposts. In Cooperstown, most of them refer to baseball. 'Left for: Baseball Hall of Fame, Baseball Museum, Major League Baseball office and Town Center.' You can have a beer in Mickey Mantle's Bar, drink watery tea in Babe Ruth's Diner, buy a miniature bat in Big League Sports. Wherever you look or turn, baseball follows you. They closed down the cinema, the waitress at my hotel told me, 'to make room for yet another gimmicky baseball shop'.

The Hall of Fame is the main drawing card, a pristine split-level, neo-classical structure of vaguely military style. Having entered through a ballpark-style turnstile, I was quickly ushered into the grand atrium ('You *must* start in the right place', I was warned). There I was greeted by a room full of austere bronze busts, neatly lined up in chronological order, beginning with Ty Cobb and Babe Ruth. Beneath the bust of every Hall of Fame player (or umpires – they can make it, too) is a breathless biographical inscription, usually outlining several statistical records. No wonder there are so many statistical subdivisions: there have to be enough records to go around the Hall of Fame. The bronzes reminded me of a cross between an Oscar and a sculpture of a Roman emperor. 'Great men them all', is very much the tone, 'and here *forever*.'

Indeed, the whole place reeks of a striving for immortality. Perhaps that is why I found it so depressing. It is as if a whole game, terrified of being forgotten, had set up monuments to itself. The D-Day museums around the Normandy beaches aren't nearly as portentous as Cooperstown's Hall of Fame. Imagine a combined creative team of Disneyland and Nike Town designing a celebrity graveyard and you have the Hall of Fame.

On the first floor, above the marble atrium and the bronze busts, is the museum proper. It begins with the story of the evolution of baseball. Under the heading 'Early Games of Ball' (note the *faux* dignity of the phrase 'Games of Ball', rather than the more run-of-the-mill term 'ballgames') the following appears:

In the beginning, shortly after God created the heaven and earth, there were stones to throw and sticks to swing. Thus, while the origins of baseball are lost in antiquity, something like it went on in prehistoric civil- isations. People competed in games using round balls and straight bats around 2000 BC in Egypt as part of religious ceremonies.

Stoolball was brought to America by the Pilgrims. It had begun in England around 1300. Rounders and cricket, long-established games with specific rules, also came across the sea with our founding fathers.

Baseball, as we know it, probably had its roots in one of these early bat-and-ball games. No one knows for sure, but baseball was born in America. That we do know for sure.

Such is the essential historical outline of baseball according to the Hall of Fame: God . . . prehistory . . . sticks and stones . . . origins of baseball . . . American baseball itself. I was a little surprised that cricket and rounders even earned a mention – though, inevitably, 'no one knows for sure' about their role. But is baseball American? 'That we do know for sure.' In the midst of so much one-eyed American historical determinism, I was beginning to feel very foreign. After years of believing that intellectuals – particularly disgruntled American intellectuals – vastly overstate the absurdity of American patriotic propaganda, suddenly I could see what the Commies were on about. This, surely, was a joke? Sadly not. The only thing missing in Cooperstown is irony.

Cooperstown is not without some merit, or interesting artefacts. I shuddered at the sight of Ty Cobb's sharpened spikes, and smiled at Babe Ruth's enormous fur coat. Best of all, I savoured Ted Williams's graphic analysis of what he called 'the science of hitting'. Williams – who announced at the beginning of his career that he wished to be remembered as 'the greatest hitter who ever lived' – was once asked what percentage of pitches he hit in the various areas of the strike zone. His answer revealed the extent to which he tried to conquer batting. He created a zone-sized strike grid of base-balls, eleven high and seven wide.

Williams imagined that each ball represented the total number of pitches he received in that area of the strike zone during his career. What percentage of those pitches did he hit successfully? On each ball he wrote a percentile: up to .480 or .490 in the middle of the strike zone – in his best hitting arc – and as low as .210 or .220 on the outer corners. There can be no better testament than that to the career (and life) of Ted Williams, almost exclusively obsessed, as it has been, with hitting baseballs.

I tried to imagine (unsuccessfully) Bradman, Sobers or Tendulkar having the inclination to give each area of the pitch an average score – twenty, perhaps, for length balls on off stump, or ninety for half-volleys on leg stump. Perhaps the unpredictability of cricket bowlers and pitches, and the sense that batting is an art not a science, does not encourage such rigorous analysis.

But Cooperstown's holiest of holies is not a room full of Babe Ruth's bats or Joe DiMaggio's shirts. Set aside from the rest of the museum like an altar, up a small ramp, separated from the chaff by a new, bright green colour code, lies the statistics room. For anyone seeking to understand the culture of American sport, it is a must. The cream of the elite, baseball's crack troops, are ranked in thirty-six tables of statistics on a giant scoreboard of records. They've narrowed it down that far – down to thirty-six ways of measuring greatness.

Pitchers get eight bites at the cherry: Games Pitched, Games Won, Complete Games, Shutouts, Innings Pitched, Earned Run Average, Strikeouts, Saves. Each of those categories is further split into 'All-Time' and 'Active' players. Batters have ten shots at immortality: Games, Runs, Doubles, Home Runs, Average, Times at Bat, Hits, Triples, Runs Batted In, Stolen Bases. All of which, of course, are subdivided into 'All-Time' and 'Active'. There are also several 'clubs' in the stats temple. Pitchers can join the '200 Victory Club', batters the '300 Home Runs Club'. It reminded me of Prizegiving Day at my junior school, where there were always more cups than pupils. I reckoned that the greatest achievement of all would be to leave school without having won any prize at all.

In a way the attention to detail at Cooperstown is tremendous. It illuminates the rigour of those who administer the game, and the passion of those who follow it. But not for the first time in my journey into baseball I felt there was a crucial lack of perspective. I hate people trivialising sport as if it doesn't matter. Of course it matters. But by so determinedly and humourlessly preserving the precise deeds of so many greats, the Hall of Fame succeeded only in reminding me how transient and silly sport appears when it is held up as a form of religion. Watching a 20-stone, fifteen-year-old girl take notes on Ty Cobb's career, extravagantly shaking her head in amazement at the wondrous numbers on her notepad, I felt conscious of voyeuristic hero-worship gone too far.

Give me the ramshackle but idiosyncratic Lord's museum any day. There are certain things about England you never appreciate until you go abroad. Dignified public ceremonies, patriotism without too much flag-waving, an ability to celebrate with understatement. And the first time I went round Lord's – while Middlesex were depriving Kent of the County

Championship in September 1988 – I rem[...]
this really *it*, the home of cricket? The m[...]
randomness of the old bats, caps and stu[...] very
impressive at the time.

But standing in Cooperstown's Hall of Fame, among so
much clinically ordered excellence and so many criteria of
brilliance, it seemed to me that Lord's had struck just the
right note. In not trying too hard, it had acquired all the more
resonance.

Having stood at the altar, I was suddenly made aware of a
much broader phenomenon: the Church of Baseball. It is a
flourishing denomination, as anyone who has watched Ken
Burns' epic nine-episode (one for each 'inning'), eighteen-
hour video *Baseball* will know. Burns, a highly respected
historian and film-maker, has made (among others) vast doc-
umentaries about what he considers to be the three most
important components of American identity: the Civil War,
jazz and baseball. In *Baseball*, Burns interviewed all the game's
most eminent writers, broadcasters, poets and philosophers.
Mario Cuomo, the persuasive governor of New York, and
one-time minor league baseball player, set the tone:

> The idea of coming together. In baseball, you do that
> all the time. You can't win it alone. You can be the best
> pitcher in baseball but somebody has to get you a run
> to win the game. It is a community activity. You need
> all nine people helping one another. I love bunt plays.
> I love the idea of the bunt. I love the idea of the sacri-
> fice. Even the word is good. That's Jeremiah. That's

thousands of years of baseball wisdom. You find your
own good in the good of the whole. You find your
own individual fulfilment in the success of the
community – the Bible tried to teach you that and
didn't teach you. Baseball did.

Ah! The *individual within the group* – never heard of that
before, have we? There are no equivalent situations, of
course, in orchestras, cricket teams or rowing eights! Only
baseball can teach you about being a team player and the
broader context . . .

Cuomo was far from being alone. Baseball's great and good
were all at it. Baseball is unique, they agreed. As a form of
experience, baseball 'connects' (*connect* recurs in Burns' video
almost as often as the word 'American') people uniquely to
America by dint of its unique American-ness – which, of
course, is like saying something is true because it is true. And
among games, baseball is qualitatively the greatest because it
embraces individualism within the context of the whole. That
is the relentlessly on-message view of *Baseball*.

In a strong field, Roger Angell, of the *New Yorker*, took the
award for most gracious evangelist. 'It's like joining an enormous family with ancestors and forebears and famous
stories . . . And it's a privilege. And the people who tell me
they hate baseball, they're out of baseball – they sound bitter
about it. But I think they sense what they are missing. I think
that they feel that there's a terrible loss that they're not in on
which is a terrible loss. And I'm sorry for them.'

You don't follow cricket, then, Roger? I feel so sorry for
you.

Similar claims have been made on baseball's behalf throughout its rich literature. As the historian John Thorn put it: 'Baseball is the missing piece of the puzzle, the part that makes us whole. While America is about breaking apart, baseball is about connecting. America is a lonely nation in which culture, class, ideology, and creed fail to unite us; baseball is the tie that binds. In this daunting land of opportunity, a man must venture forth to make his own way. Baseball is about coming home.' Thorn was surely closer to the truth when he wrote, 'one of the ways in which baseball and America manifest hope for the future is to lie about the reality of the present, or at least delude themselves'.

There is something about baseball that makes normally sedate writers become ecstatically *ex cathedra*. Peter Palmer likened the baseball 'box score' to St Peter's 'Book of Life'. Melvin Adelman even contended that baseball took precedence over cricket in late nineteenth-century America because in baseball (unlike in cricket) you couldn't carry on batting indefinitely. Thus 'baseball's structure expressed America's commitment to equal opportunities as each batter is afforded roughly the same number of at-bats regardless of success'. Michael Novak's *The Joy Sports* went further. Baseball, he concluded, was 'born out of the enlightenment and the philosophies so beloved of Jefferson, Madison and Hamilton . . . Designed as geometrically as the city of Washington . . . orderly, reasoned, judiciously balanced . . . a Lockean game, a kind of contract theory in ritual form.' Novak likened baseball to the Constitution, integrating a system of checks and balances, with the umpire as the judiciary, the batters as executives, and the fielders 'a congress checking the power of the hitters'.

Leader of the baseball apostles, though, is Thomas Boswell. In his serious essay 'The Church of Baseball', which is so reverential that it would be impossible to parody, Boswell remembers how his mother used to go to baseball matches in the same spirit in which she went to church. 'She sought places with an egalitarian bias – places where everyone started off equal, elbow to elbow. In church, everyone was equal before God. In the ball park, a fan, of course, is a fan is a fan.' She was a nice person, Mrs Boswell. But she was also a high-powered woman, who wrote speeches for congressmen and senators during the day, but, at a baseball night game, 'give her a Coke, a pack of cigarettes, and people to watch and she was tickled'. In her sixties, Mrs Boswell was taken seriously ill and lapsed into a coma. When she recovered, her first request was to take a long, slow trip by car. She chose the shrine of Cooperstown as her destination, to watch the induction of one of her favourite players into the Hall of Fame. There she could observe life after death:

Baseball believes that a man writes his name in the book of life and that what he writes, no matter how small, holds its space forever and will never be edited out of existence no matter how cumbersome *The Baseball Encyclopedia* (now up to 2857 pages) might someday become. These days, ballplayers call the major leagues the show. They say they have made 'the show'. But, as they age, what they discover is that they made the Book.

To many followers, baseball really is a religion – complete with quasi-divine analogies, holy artefacts, apostles (journalists), high priests (writers), chapels (school baseball diamonds), churches (minor league ball parks), cathedrals (major league stadia) and a resting place on earth for those immortals now gone to heaven (the Hall of Fame in Cooperstown).

Why did a simple bat and ball game inspire such an excessive and patriotic brand of worship? Perhaps because baseball became the national pastime when America was a fledgling nation, struggling for its own voice and self-confidence.

That is also why baseball's Americanophile self-worship seemed so discordant when I visited Cooperstown on that snowy day in December 2000. What was there to worry about? America had long been the world's only superpower, and baseball had never been richer or more widespread. Neither looked in need of such improbable metaphysics any longer.

Perhaps if I had gone a year later, after 11 September 2001, when America really did feel under threat, I might have felt differently.

Has any other game ever inspired such extravagant theorising? Cricket once did. The claims made on behalf of cricket are so famous that they scarcely need repeating. They are entwined with a perception of English identity – 'playing with a straight bat', 'just not cricket', 'more than just a game'. Those unlikely ideals have inspired genuinely remarkable selflessness and thinly veiled hypocrisy in roughly equal measure. Some point to those knights of the game as justification for cricket's self-improving rhetoric; others have shopping lists full of smug villains.

Cricket's great historical myths fall into three main categories: that it was essentially English and rural, that it was always a civilising force, that it was played for self-improvement not profit. Cricket's mythology – like baseball's – requires us to believe in progression from rustic innocence to a golden age, followed by decline. This decline is thought to reflect a broader modern collapse of moral fibre.

Considering that the modern game's fan (and talent) base has moved so distinctly towards the subcontinent, it seems ironic how much was once made of cricket's Englishness. The encomiastic historian, the Reverend James Pycroft articulated a common view in 1851 when he argued that cricket was 'essentially Anglo-Saxon'. 'Foreigners,' he added, 'have rarely, very rarely, imitated us. The English settlers and residents everywhere play at cricket; but of no single club have we ever heard dieted either with frogs, sauerkraut or macaroni.' Neville Cardus took xenophobia a stage further: 'Where the English language is unspoken there can be no real cricket, which is to say the Americans have never excelled at the game.'

The Victorian Charles Box, in a spirit that would have appealed to leader writers at the *Sun*, concurred. 'The effete inhabitants of cloudless Italy, Spain and Portugal,' he scoffed, 'would sooner face a solid square of British infantry than an approaching ball from the sinewy arms of a first-class bowler. Instead of the bat, their backs would be turned for the purpose of stopping it.' You can see why other countries – albeit rarely the butts of Box's joke – used to enjoy beating England so much.

The idea that cricket was once removed from the muddied world of bucks, betting and self-aggrandisement is even more laughable. The first recorded cricket match, at Coxheath, Kent, in 1646, includes a reference to betting. The opening county fixture between, sad though I am to admit it, Kent and London in 1719, ended in a lawsuit because of disputed financial payments. By 1751 Old Etonians vs England was played for £1500, with £20,000 at risk in side bets.

The myth that cricket enjoyed an unsullied golden age of innocence has about as much validity as the idea that the clocks don't move and a Coke costs a nickle in Cooperstown. Even the division between professionals and amateurs was not always what it seemed. As the professional A. E. Knight, bemoaning the practice of 'shamateurism', put it in 1906, 'many an "amateur" so termed, playing in county cricket is more heavily remunerated than an accredited "professional" player.' A. W. Carr, captain of England and Nottinghamshire during the 1920s, was also unusually honest in his appraisal of cricketers. They were not, he wrote, 'clean-limbed noble Englishmen, on the verge of sprouting wings. No, no, a thousand times no!'

What of cricket being the beacon of civility and sword of honour? Again, sometimes, perhaps, it was. But the Indian prince K. S. Ranjitsinhji probably went too far when he argued that cricket was 'one of the greatest contributions which the British people have made to the cause of humanity'. He was, of course, feeding English myths to the English, who liked to agree with Tom Brown in believing that cricket was more than a game, it was 'an institution'. A century later,

Neville Cardus, with the air of one producing a rabbit from a hat, surmised:

> It is far more than a game, this cricket . . . If everything else in this nation of ours were lost but cricket – her Constitution and the laws of England of Lord Halsbury – it would be possible to reconstruct from the theory and practice of cricket all the eternal Englishness which has gone to the establishment of that Constitution and the laws aforesaid.

To the ultimate renaissance man, C. B. Fry, cricket was 'a cult and a philosophy inexplicable to the *profanum vulgus* . . . the merchant-minded . . . and the unphysically intellectual.' Not just a game, then? Certainly not. It was the agent of civility around the world and guarantor of harmony and unity at home. Even the notable historian G. M. Trevelyan was sucked in. 'If the French noblesse had been capable of playing cricket with their peasants,' he wrote, 'their chateaux would never have been burnt.'

Lest we get too carried away, it is worth remembering another of cricket's apologists. Who said: 'Cricket? It civilises people and makes gentlemen. I want everyone to play cricket.' Robert Mugabe, of all people. The point being that a sport, *per se*, cannot have a morality. Sportsmen can, of course, and the prevailing climate and culture of their sport will affect them. But bats and balls and wickets, as David Watkin argued in reference to buildings in *Architecture and Morality*, are ethically neutral. What we do with or inside them is another matter.

The idea that cricket exists in a separate sporting realm is, of course, scarcely gaining momentum. It would be cowardly, at the beginning of the twenty-first century, to spend too much energy attacking ideas long since dismantled by the dubious forces of political correctness and post-colonialism. I bring up these colourful cricketing myths, so beloved of previous generations of Englishmen, only because I was reminded of them when I encountered some of the extraordinary claims made by Americans about baseball.

When Herbert Hoover said that, 'Next to religion, baseball has furnished a greater impact on American life than any other institution', he sounded like an Edwardian gentleman cricketer. The two games have been uniquely susceptible to such philosophising. There is one big difference: English cricket has long since conceded that other games (not to mention other countries) might be of some merit. We laugh – perhaps sometimes too heartily – at our sport's former follies. In baseball, they're still at it, toeing the American party line. It is touching, in a way, that they haven't grown out of it. It is also one of the few respects in which baseball's evolution lags distinctly behind cricket.

Sir Derek Birley was surely right when he wrote that cricket is 'a game, a good one and one that should be played properly, but a game all the same'. That, he added, 'seems not only a more honest appraisal of the realities but a more perceptive appreciation of the significance of games in human life'.

I suspect that many of the spiritual, ethical and pseudo-religious trimmings that have been attached to cricket and, in different ways, to baseball, may derive from a misplaced sense of embarrassment. It can't be *just the game* that we enjoy so much, people have said to themselves; there must be more to it. Hence the wobbly metaphysics.

And there is always more to it than 'just the game'. There is the pageantry, the aesthetic, the ambience, the scene, the whole cultural backdrop. All that is a natural part of any sport's appeal. In time, I came to appreciate much of baseball's Americana. But there is a limit to how much a game can be made to represent or embody; and in the case of cricket and baseball, that point was reached long ago.

15

AN ENGLISHMAN
IN YANKEE STADIUM

I've been watching baseball for three years now and following it for two, and discordant days like that one in Cooperstown are getting rarer. The more I watch, the more I forgive baseball its excesses. I have begun to suspect that my enjoyment of baseball might even be linked to a broader affection for America. The implied celebration of American identity is an undeniable part of the game's psychological appeal, and so long as that celebration does not cross the line into absurdity, I am increasingly happy to buy into the whole emotional package.

Like many Brits who spend a lot of time in America, I have begun to feel a sense of blurred national identity. Initially I had been amused by America's emotional self-expression. All those flags outside rural houses, the endless anthem singing, the whole God-Bless-America phenomenon. It was good writer's material, and fun in a kitsch kind of way, but I generally hung on to my English sense of irony and detachment.

Then suddenly I realised I *was* enjoying it all – the anthem, the flags, the generosity of spirit, the casual warmth of Americans. It was no longer an interesting study of a different way of doing things, it was genuinely affecting. The British journalist Andrew Sullivan wrote about that Anglo-American feeling in the *New York Times Magazine*. 'I remember the first time I got a lump in my throat singing 'The Star-Spangled Banner'. It took me completely by surprise. My attachment to my new country had taken shape and form without my even knowing it, until I found myself tearing up in a routine ritual of patriotism.'

Sullivan's conversion is far deeper than mine – he has lived in America for twenty years, whereas I have never properly lived outside England for more than a few months at a time. But I know that feeling only too well. It is inspiring and disarming in equal measure.

It happened to me in Yankee Stadium in Game 5 of the 2001 World Series. The whole series had been unusually poignant. It was the Mets, as we have seen, not the Yankees, who initially became most closely associated with New York's rehabilitation after 11 September. But when the Mets were eliminated at the end of the regular season, part of the spirit they had generated passed to the Yankees.

The Yankees faced the Arizona Diamondbacks in the World Series. God knows how the Yankees even made it that far. They had no right to win either the divisional play-offs or the American League championship. They were often outplayed, but got by on the strength of their legendary spirit, belief and perhaps – if you believe in such things – the sense that they were 'doing it for the city'.

It couldn't prevent them losing the first two games of the

World Series to the Diamondbacks, whose two ace pitchers, Randy Johnson and Curt Shilling, proved almost unhittable. The Yankees won Game 3 with a little to spare, but looked dead and buried in Game 4 when they were 4-2 down with only one out left in the ninth innings. After a post-season full of miraculous last-minute comebacks, the Yankees took things to an entirely new fairytale level when Tino Martinez hit a bottom-of-the-ninth two-run home run off pitcher Byung-Hyun Kim. Of all the last chance saloons, that is the final one. They then wrapped things up in extra innings play.

Having levelled the series at 2-2, the Yankees had one more home game before completing the best-of-seven series in Arizona. Regardless of the result, it was New York's chance to celebrate an unprecedentedly emotional autumn of baseball.

My seats were in the middle of a particularly vocal group of Yankees fans. But the whole stadium was almost exclusively full of home fans, unlike Shea the previous year where as many as a quarter of the fans were Yankees not Mets fans. This was a night of tribal simplicities not bi-partisanship.

The problem was that the Yankees couldn't hit anything. Their bats had been muted all series, doing just enough to keep them in contention. In Game 5, they were completely scoreless and 2-0 down at the bottom of the ninth with only one out left. This was asking for one miracle too many. When Scott Brosius came to bat it seemed ludicrous to believe that he might duplicate Martinez's feat of the previous night. Most spectators thought so. A few unbelievers even left early.

Brosius's now famous home run, again off the luckless Kim, seemed to happen in slow motion. Disbelieving fans mutely followed the arc of the ball. Surely this couldn't be happening.

Not twice. Surely it would fall short of the fence, into the waiting glove of the leftfielder, or curve out of bounds. Surely.

It didn't. It cleared the fence and stayed in play – two runs, game tied. It was then that the explosion of primal emotion came. It was simply beyond belief. How many fairytales can you cope with?

In seat B2, strange things were happening even to this Yankee-averse baseball convert. I had spent the whole post-season trying – and failing – to support the Yankees. They were still anti-Mets to me. But as I watched Brosius's hit sail into leftfield I was amazed to feel unmixed elation. A Yankees fan? This was going too far.

But it wasn't the Yankees I was supporting. Somehow the emotion of the night – the vast ripped and battered flag in centrefield that had been recovered from the rubble of the World Trade Center, the Harlem Boys' Choir's rendition of 'God Bless America', the sense that the city needed something great to happen that night – had overcome all my English, ironic and pro-Mets prejudices. When Alfonso Soriano hit the now apparently inevitable game-winning run in extra-innings play, it felt like the last act of a pre-ordained script. Destiny, dynasty, never-say-die – call it what you will.

There is something very special about being in an exuberantly happy crowd. Total strangers jumped into each other's arms or gave wildly enthusiastic high fives. They played Frank Sinatra's 'New York, New York' six or seven times after the game. And after more than four hours of baseball on a chilly November night, most of the 60,000 fans stayed to sing along.

Winding my way down the exit tunnel, dozens of people

coming the other way trailed an arm inside the iron railings that separated the different levels just to shake hands or give high fives to random strangers. The crowd eventually moved towards the subway where they continued to sing 'New York, New York' in packed subway carriages on the way downtown. It's not often, as a fan or a player, you get that 'I was there' feeling.

At the risk of contradicting my critique of Cooperstown, that night in Yankee Stadium, as I sang along with New Yorkers who had been so in need of something to distract and something to celebrate, and having witnessed baseball provide that opportunity, I felt more forgiving of the way Americans rally around their own inventions. Institutions like baseball, in a sense, are the American equivalent of a monarchy: they are invested with much more meaning in moments of crisis. It all seemed more justifiable on 1 November 2001.

But it wasn't the first time I had felt that instinctive emotional response to a peculiarly American experience. A few months earlier I had watched a video of Lou Gehrig's farewell to Yankee Stadium in 1939. Where 1 November 2001 had been an ecstatic night, Gehrig's farewell was an overwhelmingly sad affair. I had watched it alone, and so my response was inevitably very different, but it recognisably came from the same well of Americanophile emotion.

Gehrig was one of the greatest Yankee legends of all: a powerful hitter, a relentless competitor, a club stalwart. He was at the Yankees' core for a decade and a half.

But at the age of thirty-five Gehrig had suddenly begun to play like an old man, dropping easy balls, missing again and again at-bat, sliding his feet along rather than lifting them. Something was terribly wrong. In the locker room after one game, Gehrig fell while putting on his trousers. His team-mates looked on as he struggled to his feet.

He had played in a record 2130 consecutive games and earned himself the nickname the Iron Horse. Giving up seemed impossible; but so was letting down his team-mates. So at Detroit on 2 May 1939, he walked slowly from the dugout and handed the umpire a Yankee line-up. For the first time in fourteen years it did not include his name.

Shortly afterwards, his doctor confirmed that Gehrig had the progressive and incurable disease amyotrophic lateral sclerosis. Gehrig made his doctor explain the disease in a public letter so that no one would think him a quitter.

The 4 July 1939 was Lou Gehrig Appreciation Day at Yankee Stadium. Gehrig's old and new Yankee team-mates, along with 62,000 fans, turned up to hear the speeches and tributes. Joe McCarthy, the Yankees' manager, was afraid Gehrig might collapse; even standing was difficult now that he couldn't straighten his spine.

At first Gehrig appeared too moved to say anything, but he eventually stepped up to the microphone:

Fans, for the past two weeks you have been reading
about a bad break I got. Yet today I consider myself the
luckiest man on the face of the earth. I have been in
ball parks for seventeen years and I have never
received anything but kindness and encouragement
from you fans. Look at these grand men. Which of you
wouldn't consider it the highlight of his career just to

associate with them for even one day? Sure I'm lucky.
Who wouldn't have considered it an honour to have
known Jacob Ruppert? Also, the builder of baseball's
great empire, Ed Barrow? To have spent six years with
that wonderful little fellow, Miller Huggins? Then to
have spent nine years with that outstanding leader,
that smart student of psychology, the best manager in
baseball today, Joe McCarthy? Sure, I'm lucky. When
the New York Giants, a team you would give your right
arm to beat and vice versa, sends you a gift, that's
something. When everybody down to the grounds-
keepers and those boys in white coats remember you
with trophies, that's something. When you have a
father and a mother who work all their lives so that
you can have an education and build your body, it's a
blessing. When you have a wife who has been a tower
of strength and shown more courage than you dreamed
existed, that's the finest I know. So I close in saying
that I might have had a bad break, but I have an awful
lot to live for.

Gehrig's number four was retired. Mayor La Guardia gave
Gehrig a job as a parole commissioner and he did his best to
do it, even though he could no longer tie his own shoelaces
and his wife had to help him hold the pen so that he could
sign his name. Gehrig died on Monday, 2 June 1941, only two
years after he played the last of his 2170 consecutive games.
    I cried the first time I saw the footage of Lou Gehrig
Appreciation Day somewhere in the middle of Ken Burns'
eighteen-hour baseball film. Everyone does, I soon found out.

Even now, having seen it dozens of times, it never fails to move me.

Aside from the personal tragedy, the swift decline of a great player and the physical disintegration of a wonderful athlete, the emotion of that day in Yankee Stadium tapped into a broader American vein. It is a vein that doesn't suit everyone. If you were particularly sceptical of American sentimentality, and suspicious of their predisposition to manufacture hope in the most traumatic circumstances, you might have been disturbed by the spontaneous outpouring of sympathy and applause which burst from the stands as Gehrig finished his speech.

You might have been concerned by the obvious reverence in the stadium for 'just a ballplayer'. You might even have been unconvinced when Babe Ruth, who had feuded with Gehrig for years, rushed forward to embrace him. You might have considered the day's uniquely American feel to be a form of national propaganda: an all-American hero feeding comforting myths to the Americans.

Or instead, like me, you might have marvelled at Gehrig's grace and magnanimity. You might have found his refusal to countenance introspection and self-pity inspiring. You might have sensed that in such moments sport can have a meaning far beyond its normal scope. You might have hoped that, in such circumstances, you too would have said something similar – and suspected that you wouldn't have managed it.

You might have felt that even among American sports, only baseball, and perhaps only baseball in New York, has such communal meaning. It was clear the man mattered. You might have recognised that few other peoples are so adept at displaying their emotions without tripping over into parody or self-mockery. The American antipathy towards ironic detachment (itself an overstated phenomenon) has its upside. Lou Gehrig Appreciation Day was an example.

I do not always feel so uncritical. In different circumstances, I have often been disturbed by overstated Americana. But Gehrig's memorial, I think, was America at its best. It was full of hope, courage and generosity of spirit. He was modest, but not falsely self-deprecating. And then, perhaps most important of all, there was the use of language. The words flowed with that simple but rhetorical force which, at its best, is so distinct to the American voice. There were no neatly turned sentences or insightful revelations. But it added up to a profound cumulative effect.

I had many other experiences similar to watching Gehrig's speech or being at Yankee Stadium on 1 November. Those are just the two most memorable. But some things had definitely changed in the intervening months between the day I watched Ken Burns' film and the night I went to the Bronx, not only in my attitude to baseball, but also in the whole relationship between Britain and America.

In crises, some things clarify. It might sound trite to find good news in the aftermath of 11 September, but if there is any it may reside in a closer Anglo-American relationship. In a sense, I saw both sides of the equation: I was in England on 11 September, and in America in the aftermath. The instinctive British sympathy for America's suffering was obvious; so was America's gratefulness for that sympathy.

At the level of international diplomatic relations, the British support of America in its time of crisis was obviously helpful. It had enabled America to behave as though it was not entirely alone. It helped America to deflate the charge that its 'war against terror' was unilateral. 'The Brits are coming . . . the Brits are coming' ran one electronic billboard in Penn Station, New York, the day it was announced that SAS troops were ready to go into Afghanistan.

Even more importantly it helped America to *feel* it was not entirely alone. What struck me among my American friends was how instinctive their response was to British support. It wasn't only gratitude; it was also relief. At least some people don't hate, envy or resent us, they seemed to be thinking.

All the better, too, that the British people's sympathetic response to 11 September was a groundswell of popular feeling rather than intellectual posturing. In fact, it ran contrary to the resolutely anti-American views of much of the British intelligentsia.

Americanophobia has, after all, long been a popular and versatile parlour game among British intellectuals. Until relatively recently, when the EU took over as the bogeyman, it was the conservative right who led the charge against these vulgar people who not only helped undermine our empire with their dangerous ideas about democracy but also debased the quality of our beloved English language. Then the intellectual left began to bang the anti-American drum. America was the land of unfettered capitalism and fiscal conservatism, as uncaring as it was relentless in its worship of success. America, as Jonathan Freedland put it, 'is a vulgar, vile monster to be kept as far away as possible, where they lack irony, invade small countries, know nothing of the world and require a credit card before they will treat the sick'.

But most ordinary British people ignored all that in the

wake of 11 September. The *Sun*'s effusively pro-American edi-
torials were probably closer to how most British people really
felt. They were genuinely knocked by 11 September – and
you don't need to be an arch-political cynic to suspect that
had Tony Blair not understood that the popular will was with
him he might not have risked his high-profile pro-American
foreign policy.

How did all this affect me, standing there in Yankee
Stadium on 1 November 2001? Only tangentially, perhaps,
but not fancifully. During my first visits to the States I generally saw the differences between Britain and America. During
my last stay, which came in the months immediately after 11
September, I became increasingly aware of the similarities
and connections.

But the conversion was not all my own. Yes, I had
immersed myself in American culture, and yes, by writing a
book about baseball I was implicitly flattering American sport
and culture; and yes, people were probably nicer to me on
that account. But it went much deeper than that. The intervening months and years between my first visit and my most
recent one may also have witnessed a more general rediscov-
ery of the depth of Anglo-American friendship. That Osama
bin Laden should have catalysed it is richly ironic.

It felt different being an Englishman in Manhattan in
October and November 2001. And that generalised sense of
connectedness with America may have helped me to lose
myself more than ever before in the pageantry of the World
Series and its implicit celebration of New York and America.
For that, at least, I am glad.

*

Shortly after flying back to England – which passed quickly enough thanks, appropriately enough, to a sentimental but strangely affecting in-flight movie about baseball – I picked up a CD I had been meaning to listen to for months. It was a recording of Colin Cowdrey's memorial service at Westminster Abbey.

I had been given a ticket for the memorial service in March 2001, but I had been on a pre-season trip with Kent in South Africa. Kent's captain Matthew Fleming had, in fact, flown back a couple of days early so that he could get to the service.

Lord Cowdrey's death prompted an extraordinary popular and journalistic response and there is little point in my trying to add to it. One thing which did strike me as I listened to that CD is the extent to which a life like his can never happen again. His long career coincided with so many changes in the relationship between England and the rest of the world: the dismantling of the Empire, the independence of the Commonwealth, the emergence of former colonies as pre-eminent cricketing world powers, the end of England's dominance of English-invented games, and the beginning of a newly democratic cricketing community. Cricket had shifted from being an English game played internationally to being an international game also played in England. And through all those transitions, Lord Cowdrey had represented a curiously lasting embodiment of 'Englishness' in an increasingly un-English world.

At one level it is foolish to compare his memorial service with Lou Gehrig Appreciation Day at Yankee Stadium. After all, you cannot give farewell speeches at your own memorial service. You have to let others bat on your behalf. But I doubt that Lord Cowdrey would have been drawn to a Gehrig-style farewell even if it had been possible. He preferred the private word and the personal note rather than grand emotional gestures.

Many young cricketers, not just Kent players, have their Colin Cowdrey letter. I have mine. Others have something better. When Leicestershire's Darren Stevens scored a brilliant 130 at Arundel, Lord Cowdrey just happened to have popped down the road from his nearby house to watch the Arundel Festival. He gave Stevens a framed print of the ground, thanking him for 'one of the best hundreds I have seen'.

There were real acts of kindness, too, as well as nice gestures. I was once travelling across London with my cricket coffin, packed full of England U19 kit, when its handle suddenly broke. I went to buy a replacement in a sports' shop in Piccadilly. When the Indian sales assistant found out I played for Kent, his eyes lit up. 'Oh yes, Kent, wonderful county, Colin Cowdrey played there, marvellous man. I owe everything I have to him. When I met him in India I said I wanted to play cricket in England. When I flew over here he arranged some second-team county trials and organised a club for me. And here I still am! Amazing.'

Lord Cowdrey's seemingly 'English' persona did not preclude him from being liked elsewhere. Many of his greatest fans, in fact, came from other cricketing nations. And it was the internationalism as much as the nostalgia that many people remember about the memorial service. There were representatives – among them the greatest living player, Sir Garfield Sobers – from every cricketing nation. 'We had to share our father,' as Chris Cowdrey said in his address, 'with the rest of the world.' The loss was more than just England's.

How much the man was like the game in that respect. The miracle of 'English' sports is that they are so loved around the world. After so much praise about baseball's American vein, it is worth considering the capacity of English sports for international outreach. Americans are usually surprised that cricket, which they consider the most idiosyncratic and insular of English games, has spread so broadly and deeply into several continents and countless countries.

One last generalised abstraction. Perhaps cricket's ability to adapt far beyond its nationalist origins is not untypical of British institutions in general. It is no longer fashionable to believe that the Empire had much lasting international benevolence. But in one respect it was unique: in its capacity to retain amicable sporting links with its former colonies.

That is not, after all, a familiar pattern. As the historian Harold Perkin put it, admittedly with a slightly rhetorical turn of phrase: 'Can we imagine any other empires in which the successor states played games against the imperial power? Would the Franks, Vizigoths or Huns have played football with the Romans – except maybe with their heads?'

So much for the big picture. At a more personal level, I think I found listening to that memorial service all the more moving because I had just returned from a voyage into another sport and another culture. It certainly reminded me that, despite my newfound affection for America, I am just as English and just as in love with cricket as I always have been.

Ed
Plagin's